Mirza Tasnime Saeec, Ghofrani Jahromi

Infinity Plot And It,s Applications 2016 [Last Update Date (4 10 1395)] 004

Mirza Tasnime Saeed, Ghofrani Jahromi

Infinity Plot And It,s Applications 2016 [Last Update Date (4 10 1395)] 004

ISBN/EAN: 9783744651493

Printed in Europe, USA, Canada, Australia, Japan

Cover: Foto ©Paul-Georg Meister /pixelio.de

More available books at **www.hansebooks.com**

In The Name Of Allah,
Most Gracious, Most Merciful.

Article Title :

Infinity Plot And It,s Applications

Digest Description Of Miniatoric Infinity Plot Concept :

- If either of the range end points of the horizontal range contains +-infinity, an infinity plot is generated.

- An infinity plot is obtained by transforming -infinity .. infinity to $-Pi/2..Pi/2$ by a transformation that approximates arctan. This is a nice way of getting the entire picture of f(x) on the display.

- Such a graph, although distorted near x = -infinity and infinity, contains a lot of information about the features of f(x).

**The Article Is A Gift
From The GOD
To All The Believers In GOD**

**Do Not Forget The Ordained Prayer To GOD
Because Of This Great Manifest Signs Of The GOD.**

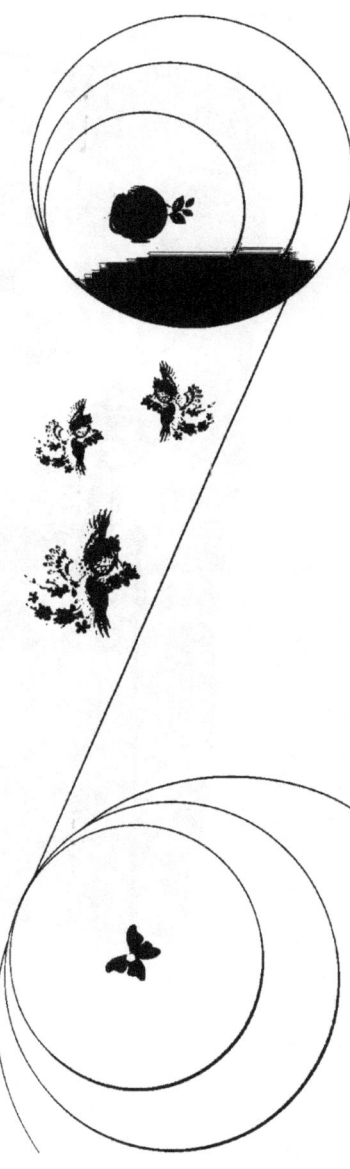

In The Name
Most Gracious
Most Merciful

Introduction

Try finding the limit of the following function using Mathematica Software, which is known as the most powerful CAS "Computer Algebra System".

$$f(x) = \frac{[x]}{x}, \quad [x] = intg(x) \quad ([x] = n \leftrightarrow n \leq x \leq n+1, n \in Z)$$

Intg=Function[{x},If[IntegerPart[x]>=0,IntegerPart[x],IntegerPart[x]-1]];

You will observe that Mathematica is unable to solve the limit.

In this article we will develop methods to find such limits, one method is graphical and it is plotting the function as x is varying in the range $-\infty < x < +\infty$. We name such plots as *Infinity Plots*. Such Plots are introduced in Maple Software But there is no extended explanation how we can do this .(I searched the internet to find a solution and finally I found a method). And the other method will be analytical.

Maple description about Infinity Plots :

Calling Sequence
plot(f, h, v, options)

Parameters

f(x) - acceptable function
h   - horizontal range
v   - vertical range (optional)

Description

. If either of the range end points of the horizontal range contains +-infinity, an infinity plot is generated.

. An infinity plot is obtained by transforming -infinity .. infinity to   by a transformation that approximates ArcTan. This is a nice way of getting the entire picture of f(x) on the display. Such a graph, although distorted near x = -infinity and infinity, contains a lot of information about the features of f(x).

. Because the view is already determined for infinity plots, the view option has no effect.

Example :

$$plot\left(\frac{1}{x}, x = -\infty .. \infty, labels = ["x", "y"]\right)$$

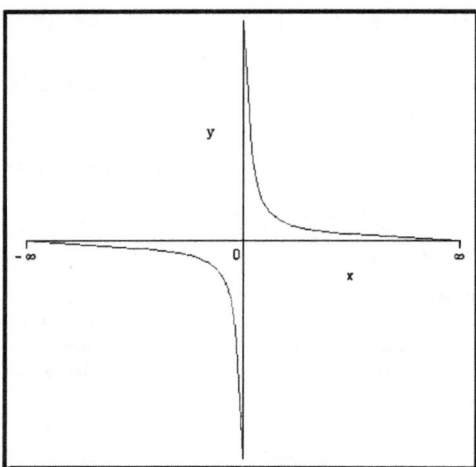

There are also other situations where these methods is helpful, they are as follows :

- Comparing the speed of different functions in growing to infinity.
- Finding the finite number of roots of a function graphically as x is varying at the range $-\infty < x < +\infty$.
- Plotting the asymptote of functions.
- Developing some codes to find the finite number of roots of functions using the Kronecher – Picard Theory.
- Developing a method to find the finite number of infinities of the function.
- Developing a method to find the Absolute maximum and minimum of functions in the domain $(-\infty, +\infty)$.
- 3D Infinity plots

- Developing some codes to find the solutions of system of nonlinear equations as the variables are changing in the range of $-\infty < x < +\infty$.

THEORY OF INFINITY PLOTS

When plotting a function if either the range end points of horizontal range contains ± infinity, an Infinity plot is generated.
Suppose that we have the function f(x) and we want to infinity plot it. We can use the following transformation to get the entire picture of f(x) on the display.

The transformation is :

$$ArcTan\left(f(Tan(x))\right) \qquad D_f = \left[-\frac{\pi}{2}, \frac{\pi}{2}\right] \quad , \quad R_f = \left[-\frac{\pi}{2}, \frac{\pi}{2}\right]$$

If this transformation is plotted as x vary at the range $-\frac{\pi}{2} \leq x \leq +\frac{\pi}{2}$ the *f(x)* will be depicted on the display for x varying at the range $-\infty < x < +\infty$.

Infinite plots are useful to inspect the behavior of one or more functions as $\to \pm\infty$. Scaling in both axes is not linear ; if the function to be plotted is oscillating for high $|x|$-values , the details are not shown correctly . In other words , Infinity plot is not suitable for plotting alternative functions. Note that it doesn,t make any sense to plot "Infinit" plots together with normal plots in the same graph ,since scaling is linear in normal plots , while this is not true in "Infinite" plots. Therefore we can not use "Infinity" plots together with the normal plots in the same graph.

Here is some examples generated using Mathematica Software . To produce the plots two Mathematica statements are used , "Function" statement and "Plot" statement.

Function Statement [1] :
Function [*body*] or *body*& is a pure function. The formal parameters are # (or #1), #2, etc.
Function [*x*, *body*] is a pure function with a single formal parameter *x*.
Function [{ x_1, x_2, ... }, *body*] is a pure function with a list of formal parameters.

Plot Statement [1] :
Plot [*f*, {*x*, x_{min}, x_{max} }] generates a plot of *f* as a function of *x* from x_{min} to x_{max} .
Plot [{f_1, f_2, ... }, {*x*, x_{min}, x_{max} }] plots several functions f_i.

Example 1:
$f(x) = x^2$

Mathematica Code:

```
F=Function [{x},x^2];
Plot[ArcTan[F[Tan[x]]],{x,-π/2,π/2}];
```

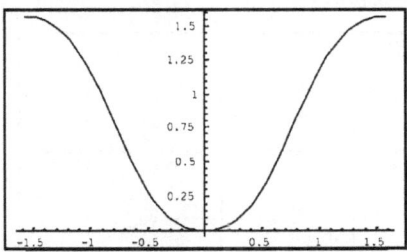

Example 2:
$f(x) = Sin(x)$

Mathematica Code:

```
F=Function [{x},Sin[x]];
Plot[ArcTan[F[Tan[x]]],{x,-π/2,π/2}];
```

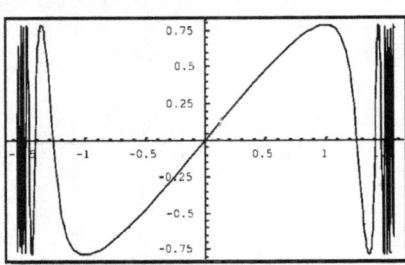

Example 3:
$$f(x) = \frac{5}{(x^2 - 4)}$$

Mathematica Code:

```
F=Function [{x},5/(x^2-4)];
Plot[ArcTan[F[Tan[x]]],{x,-π/2,π/2}];
```

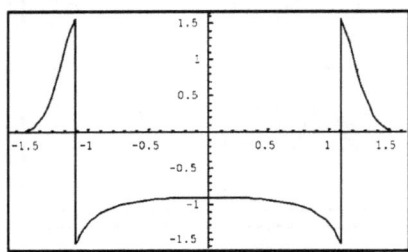

Example 4:
$f(x) = Ln(x)$
$g(x) = e^x$

Mathematica Code:

```
F=Function [{x},Log[x]];
G=Function[{x},e^x]
Plot[{ArcTan[F[Tan[x]]],ArcTan[G[Tan[x]]]},{x,-π/2,π/2}];
```

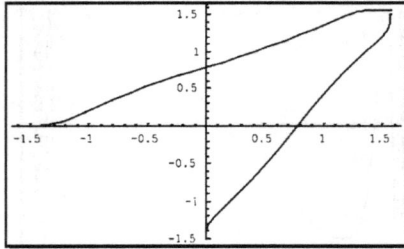

INFINITY PLOT APPLICATIONS

- **Limits Of Functions**

Several conclusions concerning the limits of the functions can be obtained using "Infinity" plots. Even there are cases where Mathematica which is known as the most powerful CAS "Computer Algebra System", can not handle, but you can use this method to find the limits of functions graphically so easily.
For Example if we try to find the limit of the following function as $x \to +\infty$ using the Mathematica Software there will be no result.

$$f(x) = \frac{[x]}{x}$$

First we should define the function $[x]$ for Mathematica :

```
Intg=Function[{x},If[IntegerPart[x]>=0,IntegerPart[x],IntegerPart[x]-1]];
```

To define the function **Intg** we have used **IntegerPart** Statement which is a build in Mathematica function, which gives the Integer Part of x, where x is the input variable.

Now we try to find the limit of the defined function "Intg" divided by X as $x \to +\infty$.

```
Limit[Intg[x]/x,x→∞]
```

The output is :

$$Lim[\frac{If[IntegerPart[x] \geq 0, IntegerPart[x], IntegerPart[x] - 1]}{x}, x \to \infty]$$

As you can see there will be no result and Mathematica was unable to handle that limit. Now we are going to try the graphical method using the "Infinity" plots.

From the Mathematics courses we know that $[x]$ as $x \to +\infty$ is equal to x. So we can guess that the limit will be simplified to :

$$\lim_{x \to +\infty} \left(\frac{x}{x}\right) = 1$$

To show that the above assumption is true we will plot $f(x) = \frac{[x]}{x}$ and $g(x) = 1$, on the same Infinity graph.

Mathematica Code:

```
Intg=Function[{x},If[IntegerPart[x]>=0,IntegerPart[x],IntegerPart[x]-1]];
F=Function[{x},Intg[x]/x];
P1=Plot[{ArcTan[F[Tan[x]]]},{x,- π /2, π /2},PlotRange→{- π /2, π /2}];
P2=Plot[{ArcTan[1]},{x,- π /2, π /2},PlotRange→{- π /2, π /2}];
P3=Plot[{ArcTan[F[Tan[x]]],ArcTan[1]},{x,- π /2, π /2},PlotRange→{- π /2, π /2}
,PlotStyle→{Thickness[.01],Dashing[{.01}]}];
```

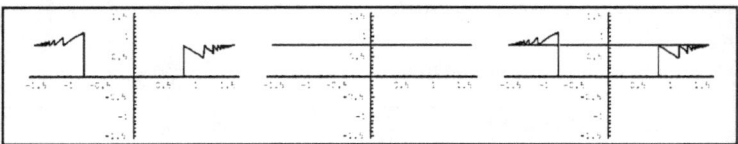

From the graph you can see that $\frac{[x]}{x}$ is getting near to 1 as $x \to \pm\infty$. So the above Conclusion was true.

Further Examples

Example 1 :

$lim_{x \to \pm\infty} \frac{5}{(x^2-4)} = ?$, $lim_{x \to -2^-} \frac{5}{(x^2-4)} = ?$, $lim_{x \to -2^+} \frac{5}{(x^2-4)} = ?$, $lim_{x \to +2^-} \frac{5}{(x^2-4)} = ?$, $lim_{x \to +2^+} \frac{5}{(x^2-4)} = ?$

Mathematica Code :

```
F=Function [{x},5/(x^2-4)];
Plot[{ArcTan[F[Tan[x]]]},{x,-π/2,π/2}];
```

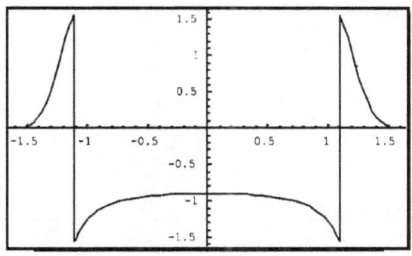

You can see that the results are :
$lim_{x \to \pm\infty} \frac{5}{(x^2-4)} = 0$
$lim_{x \to -2^-} \frac{5}{(x^2-4)} = +\infty$
$lim_{x \to -2^+} \frac{5}{(x^2-4)} = -\infty$
$lim_{x \to +2^-} \frac{5}{(x^2-4)} = -\infty$
$lim_{x \to +2^+} \frac{5}{(x^2-4)} = +\infty$

Example 2 :
$lim_{x \to 0^+} Ln(x) = ?$

Mathematica Code :

```
F=Function [{x},Log[x]];
Plot[{ArcTan[F[Tan[x]]]},{x,-π/2,π/2}];
```

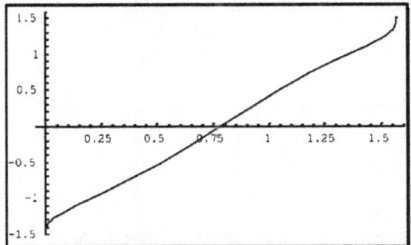

You can see that the result is $-\infty$.

Example 3:

$lim_{x \to +\infty} \frac{x^5}{e^x} = ?$

Mathematica Code:

```
F=Function[{x},x^5/e^x];
Plot[{ArcTan[F[Tan[x]]]},{x,-π/2,π/2}]
```

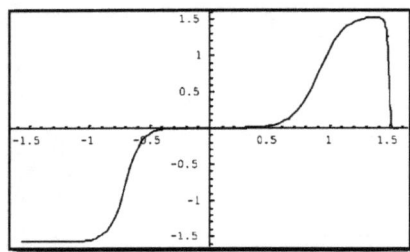

The result is 0.
Checking the result using Mathematica :

```
Limit[F[x],x-> Infinity]
```

The result is 0.

Example 4:

$lim_{x \to +\infty} (x + e^x)^{\frac{2}{x}} = ?$

Mathematica Code :

```
F=Function[{x},(x + e^x)^(2/x)];
P1=Plot[{ArcTan[F[Tan[x]]]},{x,-π/2, π /2},PlotRange→{1.4, π /2}];
P2=Plot[{ArcTan[e^2], {x,-π/2, π /2},PlotRange→{1.4, π /2}];
```

```
P3=Plot[{ArcTan[F[Tan[x]]],ArcTan[e^2], },{x,- π /2, π /2},PlotRange→{1.4, π /2},
PlotStyle→{Thickness[.001],Dashing[{.01}]}];
Show[GraphicsArray[{P1,P2,P3}]];
```

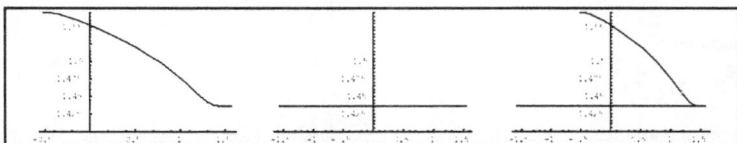

As you an see from the code and the graph the result is e^2.
Checking the result :

```
Limit[F[x],x->Infinity]
```

The result is e^2.
Example 5:
$lim_{x\to+\infty} (3x^2 + 4x)/(4x^2 + 1)$ =?

Mathematica Code :

```
F=Function[{x},(3x^2 + 4x)/(4x^2 + 1)];
P1=Plot[{ArcTan[F[Tan[x]]]},{x,- π /2, π /2},PlotRange→{- π /2, π /2}];
P2=Plot[{ArcTan[3/4]},{x,- π /2, π /2},PlotRange→{- π /2, π /2},PlotStyle→Dashing[{.01}]];
P3=Plot[{ArcTan[F[Tan[x]]],ArcTan[3/4]},{x,- π /2, π /2},PlotRange→{- π /2, π /2},
PlotStyle→{Thickness[.001],Dashing[{.01}]}];
Show[GraphicsArray[{P1,P2,P3}]];
Limit[F[x],x→-Infinity]
```

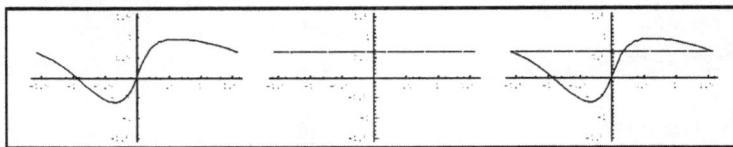

As you an see from the code and the graph the result is $\frac{3}{4}$.
Checking the result :

```
Limit[F[x],x->Infinity]
```

The result is $\frac{3}{4}$.

Example 6:
$$\lim_{x \to +\infty} \frac{x}{Ln(x) \times Ln(Ln(x))}$$

Mathematica Code :

```
F=Function[{x},x/(Ln(x)×Ln(Ln(x)))];
Plot[{ArcTan[F[Tan[x]]]},{x,-π/2, π/2},PlotRange->{-π/2, π/2}]
```

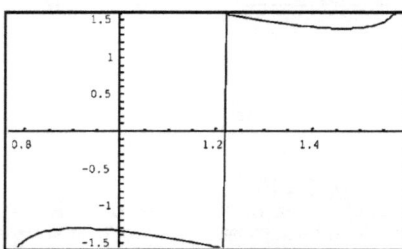

The result is $+\infty$.

Example 7 :
$$\lim_{x \to +\infty} \frac{Ln(x)}{\sqrt{-1+Ln(x)}\sqrt{1+Ln(x)}}$$

Mathematica Code :

```
F=Function[{x},Log(x)/(√(-1+Log(x))√(1+Log(x)))];
P1=Plot[{ArcTan[F[Tan[x]]]},{x,-π/2, π/2},PlotRange→{-π/2, π/2}];
P2=Plot[{ArcTan[1]},{x,-π/2, π/2},PlotRange→{-π/2, π/2},PlotStyle→Dashing[{.01}]};
```

```
P3=Plot[{ArcTan[F[Tan[x]]],ArcTan[1]},{x,-π/2, π/2},PlotRange→{-π/2, π/2},
PlotStyle→{Thickness[.001],Dashing[{.01}]}];
Show[GraphicsArray[{P1,P2,P3}]];
Limit[F[x],x→-Infinity]
```

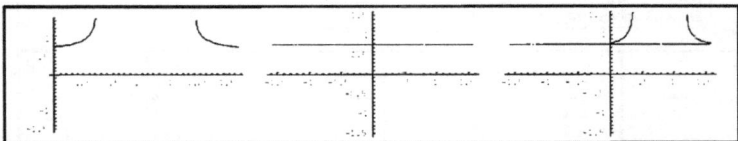

As you an see from the code and the graph the result is 1.

Example 8 :

$$\lim_{x\to+\infty} \frac{3^x - 3^{-x}}{3^x + 3^{-x}}$$

Mathematica Code :

```
F=Function[{x},(3^x-3^-x)/(3^x+3^-x)];
P1=Plot[{ArcTan[F[Tan[x]]]},{x,-π/2, π/2},PlotRange→{-π/2, π/2}];
P2=Plot[{ArcTan[-1]},{x,-π/2, π/2},PlotRange→{-π/2, π/2},PlotStyle→Dashing[{.01}]];
P3=Plot[{ArcTan[F[Tan[x]]],ArcTan[-1]},{x,-π/2, π/2},PlotRange→{-π/2, π/2},
PlotStyle→{Thickness[.001],Dashing[{.01}]}];
Show[GraphicsArray[{P1,P2,P3}]];
Limit[F[x],x→-Infinity]
```

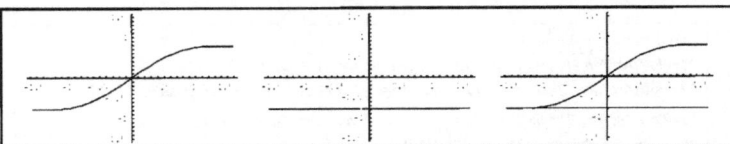

As you an see from the code and the graph the result is −1.

Example 9 :

$$\lim_{x\to+\infty}\left(\frac{x+.2}{x-.2}\right)^x$$

Mathematica Code :

```
F=Function[{x},(x+.2/x-.2)^x];
P1=Plot[{ArcTan[F[Tan[x]]]},{x,- π /2, π /2},PlotRange→{0, π /2}];
P2=Plot[{ArcTan[e^(2x.2)]},{x,-π/2, π /2},PlotRange→{0, π /2},PlotStyle→Dashing[{.01}]];
P3=Plot[{ArcTan[F[Tan[x]]], ArcTan[e^(2x.2)]}, {x,- π /2, π /2}, PlotRange→{0, π /2}, PlotStyle π
{Dashing[{1}],Dashing[{.01}]}];
Show[GraphicsArray[{P1,P2,P3}]];
```

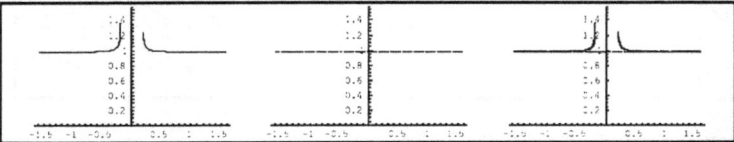

As the Code and the Graphs show the result is $e^{2\times.2}$.
Checking the result :
We know that :
$$\lim_{x\to+\infty}(1+\frac{a}{x})^{bx}=e^{ab}$$

So :

$$lim_{x\to+\infty}\left(\frac{x+.2}{x-.2}\right)^x = lim_{x\to+\infty}\left[\frac{x(1+\frac{.2}{x})}{x(1-\frac{.2}{x})}\right]^x = \frac{lim_{x\to+\infty}(1+\frac{.2}{x})^x}{lim_{x\to+\infty}(1-\frac{.2}{x})^x} = \frac{e^{.2}}{e^{-.2}} = e^{2\times.2}$$

Example 10 :
$$\lim_{x\to-\infty}\frac{2x-1}{\sqrt{3x^2+x+1}}$$

Mathematica Code :

```
F=Function[{x},(2x-1)/√(3x²+x+1) ];
P1=Plot[{ArcTan[F[Tan[x]]]},{x,-π/2, π /2},PlotRange→{- π /2, π /2}];
P2=Plot[{ArcTan[-2/√3]},{x,- π /2, π /2},PlotRange→{- π /2, π /2},PlotStyle→Dashing[{.01}]];
P3=Plot[{ArcTan[F[Tan[x]]],ArcTan[-2/√3] },{x,- π /2, π /2},PlotRange →{- π /2, π /2},
PlotStyle→{Thickness[.01],Dashing[{.01}]}];
```

```
Show[GraphicsArray[{P1,P2,P3}]];
```

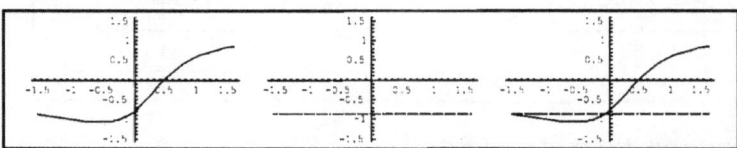

As the Code and the Graphs show the result is $\frac{-2}{\sqrt{3}}$.

Checking the result :
As we know :

$$\sqrt[n]{ax^n + bx^{n-1} + cx^{n-2} + \cdots} \sim \sqrt[n]{a}\left|x + \frac{b}{na}\right|$$

$x \to \pm\infty$

So :

$$lim_{x\to-\infty} \frac{2x-1}{\sqrt{3x^2+x+1}} = lim_{x\to-\infty} \frac{2x-1}{\sqrt{3}\left|x+\frac{1}{6}\right|} = lim_{x\to-\infty} \frac{2x-1}{-\sqrt{3}x-\frac{\sqrt{3}}{6}} = lim_{x\to-\infty} \frac{2x}{-\sqrt{3}x} = \frac{2}{-\sqrt{3}}$$

Example 11 :

$$\lim_{x\to\infty} \sqrt[3]{x^3 - 5x^2 + 2x + 1} - x$$

Mathematica Code :

```
F=Function[{x},∛(x³ − 5x² + 2x + 1) − x ];
P1=Plot[{ArcTan[F[Tan[x]]]},{x,-π/2, π /2},PlotRange→{- π /2, π /2}];
P2=Plot[{ArcTan[-5/3]},{x,- π /2, π /2},PlotRange→{- π /2, π /2},PlotStyle→Dashing[{.01}]}];
P3=Plot[{ArcTan[F[Tan[x]]],ArcTan[-5/3] ]},{x,- π /2, π /2},PlotRange →{- π /2, π /2},
PlotStyle→{Thickness[.01],Dashing[{.01}]}];
Show[GraphicsArray[{P1,P2,P3}]];
```

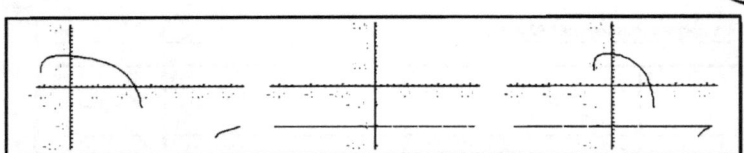

The graph and the code show that the result is $\frac{-5}{3}$.

Checking the result :
We know that :

If n is a positive Integer number and $p(x)$ is a polynomial in the following form
$p(x) = x^n + b_1 x^{n-1} + b_2 x^{n-2} + \cdots + b_{n-1} x + b_n$

Then
$$\lim_{x \to \infty} \left([p(x)]^{\frac{1}{n}} - x \right) = \frac{b_1}{n}$$

So

$$\lim_{x \to \infty} \sqrt[3]{x^3 - 5x^2 + 2x + 1} - x = \frac{-5}{3}$$

- **Comparison Between The Speed Of Different Functions In Growing To Infinity.**

It,s possible to compare the speed of different functions in growing to the Infinity using the "Infinity" plots. To do so we should plot different functions at the same time on the same graph and compare the speed of growing visually.
here is some examples showing the method.

Example :
Comparison between the speed of $(x, x^2, e^x, Ln(x))$ in growing to infinity.

Mathematica Code

```
F1=Function [{x},x];
F2=Function[{x},x^2];
F3=Function[{x}, e ^x];
F4=Function[{x},Log[x]];
Plot[{ArcTan[F1[Tan[x]]],ArcTan[F2[Tan[x]]],ArcTan[F3[Tan[x]]] ,ArcTan[F4[Tan[x]]]},{x,-π/2,π/2}];
```

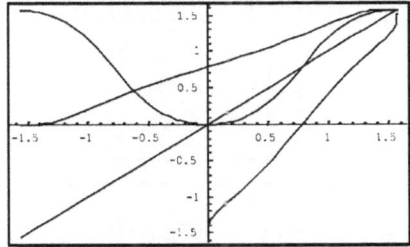

As you can see, e^x goes to $+\infty$ Faster than x^2, and x^2 goes to $+\infty$ faser than x. And $Ln(x)$ goes to $+\infty$ slowly compared to (x, x^2, e^x)

Further Examples :
We can use the above conclusion about the speed of functions to go to Infinity to determine the limits of functions.

Example 1 :

Try to find the the following limit :
$$\lim_{x \to +\infty} \frac{Ln(x)+x^2}{e^x+x} = ?$$

Matematica Code :

```
F=Function[{x},(Ln(x) + x^2)/(e^x + x)];
Plot[ArcTan[F[Tan[x]]],{x,-π/2,π/2}]
```

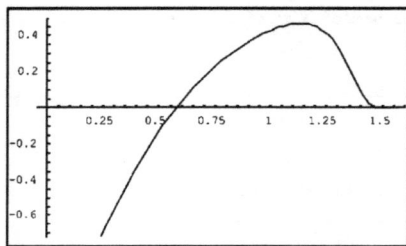

As you can see the function comes to zero as $x \to +\infty$.
Try evaluating the limit using Mathematica :

```
Limit[(Ln(x)+x^2)/(e^x+x), x → +∞]
```

The result would be zero :

```
0
```

Example 2:
Try finding the following limit :
$$\lim_{x \to +\infty} \frac{e^x}{Ln(x)} = ?$$

Mathematica Code :

```
F=Function[{x},(e^x)/(Ln(x))];
Plot[ArcTan[F[Tan[x]]],{x,-π/2,π/2}]
```

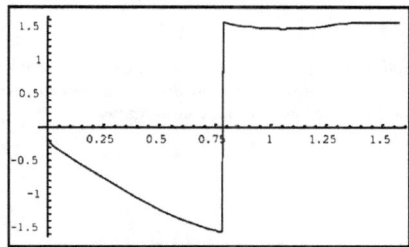

Try evaluating the limit using Mathematica :

$$\text{Limit}[\frac{e^x}{Ln(x)}, x \to +\infty]$$

The result would be ∞:

∞

As I mentioned before e^x goes to $+\infty$ faster than $Ln(x)$. So the result is true.

- **Asymptote**

Another helpful application of the Infinity Plots is to show the asymptote of functions visually. We can use the infinity plots to show the vertical, horizontal and inclined Asymptotes. We will show the method by some examples.

Vertical Asymptote

$$f(x) = \frac{\sqrt{x-2}}{x^2 - 4}$$

$x^2 - 4 = 0 \quad \rightarrow x = \pm 2$

But $x = -2$ is not Asymptote, because the Radical in the numerator of the function will have minus sign.

Mathematica Code

```
F=Function[{x}, √(x-2)/(x²-4)];
P1=Plot[{ArcTan[F[Tan[x]]]},{x,-π/2,π/2},PlotRange→{-π/2,π/2}];
P2=Plot[{0},{x,0,π/2},GridLines→{{ArcTan[2]},{0}},PlotRange→{0,π/2}]
P3=Plot[{ArcTan[F[Tan[x]]],},{x,0,π/2}, GridLines→{{ArcTan[2]},{0}},PlotRange→{0,π/2},
PlotStyle→{Thickness[.001],Dashing[{.01}]}];
Show[GraphicsArray[{{P1,P2,P3}}]];
```

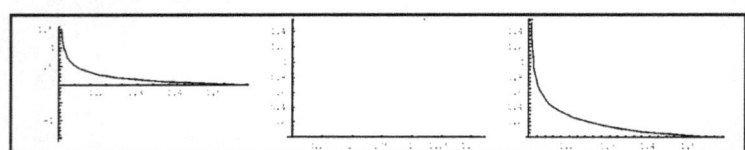

Horizontal Asymptote

$$f(x) = \frac{5 - 3x^2}{1 - x^2}$$

$lim_{x \to \mp\infty} f(x) = 3$

Also we can check the Vertical Asymptote:

$$\lim_{x\to 1^-} f(x) = +\infty \;,\; \lim_{x\to 1^+} f(x) = -\infty \;,\; \lim_{x\to -1^-} f(x) = -\infty \;,\; \lim_{x\to -1^+} f(x) = +\infty$$

Mathematica Code

```
F=Function[{x},(5-3x^2)/(1-x^2)];
P1=Plot[{ArcTan[F[Tan[x]]]},{x,-π/2, π/2},PlotRange→{-π/2, π/2}];
P2=Plot[{ArcTan[3]},{x,0, π/2},PlotRange→{-π/2, π/2},PlotStyle→Dashing[{.01}]]
P3=Plot[{ArcTan[F[Tan[x]]],ArcTan[3]},{x,-π/2, π/2},PlotRange→{-π/2, π/2},
PlotStyle→{Thickness[.001],Dashing[{.01}]}];
Show[GraphicsArray[{P1,P2,P3}]];
```

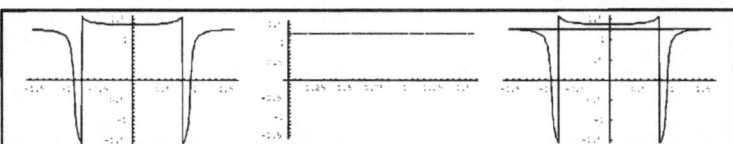

Inclined Asymptote

$$f(x) = \frac{x^3}{x^2+1}$$

$$y = ax + b \qquad a = \lim_{x\to\infty}\frac{f(x)}{x} \qquad , \qquad b = \lim_{x\to\infty}(f(x) - ax)$$

$$a = \lim_{x\to\infty}\frac{f(x)}{x} = \lim_{x\to\infty}\frac{x^2}{x^2+1} = 1$$

$$b = \lim_{x\to\infty}(f(x) - ax) = \lim_{x\to\infty}\frac{x^3}{x^2+1} - x = \lim_{x\to\infty}\frac{-x}{x^2+1} = 0$$

$$\to y = x$$

Mathematica Code

```
F=Function[{x},x^3/(x^2+1)];
G=Function[{x},x];
P1=Plot[{ArcTan[F[Tan[x]]]},{x,-π/2, π/2},PlotRange→{-π/2, π/2}];
P2=Plot[{ArcTan[G[Tan[x]]]},{x,-π/2, π/2},PlotRange→{-π/2, π/2}, PlotStyle → Dashing[{.01}]];
P3=Plot[{ArcTan[F[Tan[x]]],ArcTan[G[Tan[x]]]},{x,-π/2, π/2},GridLines→{2},PlotRange→{-π/2,
π/2},PlotStyle→{Thickness[.001],Dashing[{.01}]}];
Show[GraphicsArray[{P1,P2,P3}]];
Limit[F[x],x→-Infinity]
```

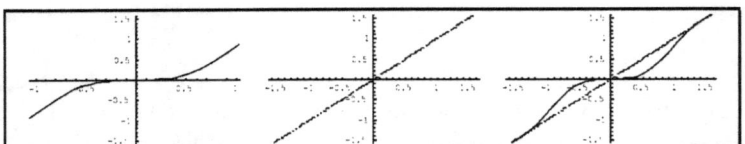

- **Finding The Finite Number Of Real Roots Of Functions Visually As x Is Varying In The Rang $-\infty < x < +\infty$.**

*I*f the function does not have an oscillating behavior as $x \to \pm\infty$ and if the number of roots of the function is finite , we can use the "Infinity" plot to visually determine the number of roots. Also it,s possible to use the Infinity transformation to find the roots .

Example 1:
We want to find the number of roots of the following function as x is varying in the range $-\infty < x < \infty$.
$sin(6 \times (x^3 - .4)) + x^4$

Mathematica Code

```
F=Function[{x},Sin[6*(x^3-.4)]+x^4];
Plot[{ArcTan[F[Tan[x]]]},{x,-π/2,π/2}]
```

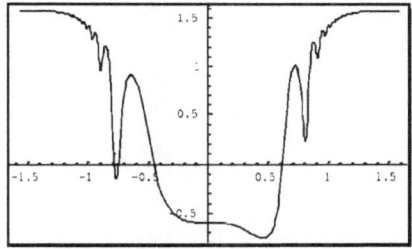

From the plot we see that the function has **4** Real roots .

Example 2:
We want to find the number of roots of the following function as x is varying in the range $-\infty < x < \infty$.

$sin(12 * x) + x^4$

Mathematica Code

```
F=Function[{x},Sin[12*x]+x^4];
Plot[{ArcTan[F[Tan[x]]]},{x,-π/2,π/2}]
```

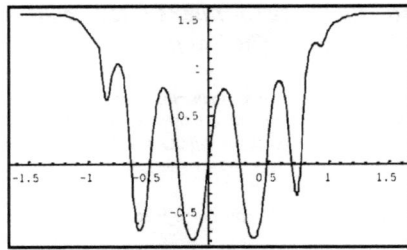

*From the plot we see that the function has **8** Real roots .*

- **Finding The Finite Real Roots of Functions Visually using Infinity Plots.**

*T*o visually find the finite real roots of the functions, first we should Infinity plot the function, then we should guess the roots using the Infinity Plot. Then we will use the Mathematica FindRoot Command to find the roots through the transformed function. We will Introduce the method through an example

Example :

Find the real roots of the following function :

$f = \tan(2 \times x) + x^3$

Solution :
The Transformed function in Mathematica code will be :

```
F=Function[x,Tan[2*x]+x^3];
G=Function[x,ArcTan[F[Tan[x]]]];
Plot[ArcTan[F[Tan[x]]],{x,-Pi/2,Pi/2}]
```

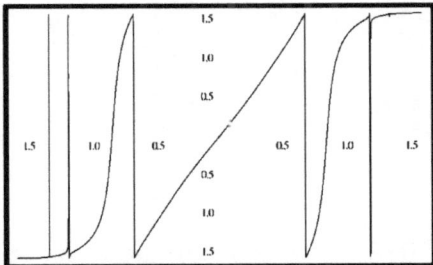

From the picture we can guess the Real Roots approximated location.

```
FindRoot[G[x] 0,{x,{0,-.81,.81}},MaxIterations→1000]
```
Result :

$$\{x \to \{0., -0.8350493275694328, 0.835049327569433\}\}$$

Real Roots :

$$\boxed{Tan[\{0, -0.835049327569433, 0.835049327569433\}]}$$

Result :

$$\{0, -1.1045808419145513, 1.1045808419145513\}$$

Testing the result using the main function :

$$\boxed{FindRoot[F[x] == 0, \{x, \{0, -1.1045808419145513, 1.1045808419145513\}\}, MaxIterations \to 1000]}$$

Result :

$$\{x \to \{0., -1.1045808419145513, 1.1045808419145513\}\}$$

So you can see that the result from the main function and from the transformed function using initial guesses optioned from the infinity plot is true .

- **Developing A Code To Find The Finite Number Of Real Roots Of Functions As x Is Varying In The Range** $-\infty < x < +\infty$

Now we are going to develop a LUA Code to determine the finite number of Real roots of functions as x is varying in the range $-\infty < x < \infty$. The procedure is that we will try to find the finite number of Real roots of the transformation function in the range $-\frac{\pi}{2} \leq x \leq \frac{\pi}{2}$. Just note that this procedure is not suitable for alternative functions in other words we can not use functions with infinite number of roots in this method.

Introduction to Lua Language :

Lua is an extension programming language designed to support general procedural programming with data description facilities. It also offers good support for object-oriented programming, functional programming, and data-driven programming. Lua is intended to be used as a powerful, light-weight scripting language for any program that needs one. Lua is implemented as a library, written in *clean* C (that is, in the common subset of ANSI C and C++).

Being an extension language, Lua has no notion of a "main" program: it only works *embedded* in a host client, called the *embedding program* or simply the *host*. This host program can invoke functions to execute a piece of Lua code, can write and read Lua variables, and can register C functions to be called by Lua code. Through the use of C functions, Lua can be augmented to cope with a wide range of different domains, thus creating customized programming languages sharing a syntactical framework. The Lua distribution includes a sample host program called lua, which uses the Lua library to offer a complete, stand-alone Lua interpreter.

Lua is free software, and is provided as usual with no guarantees, as stated in its license. The implementation described in this manual is available at Lua's official web site, www.lua.org.

Lua Codes:
Here we are going to use the Kronecker – Picard theory to find the roots of functions .
We have used the LNA "Lua Numerical Analysis " Package .

What is LNA ?
LNA stands for "Lua Numerical Analysis " ; it is a package of Numerical Analysis functions , together with several utility and plotting functions. All functions in the package are meant to be called from a program written in Cplua , which runs on a Casio Classpad 300 Calculator.

Example :
Find the roots of the following function as $x \to \pm\infty$
$f(x) = sin(6x) + x^3$

Driver Program :

```
require("LNAplot/PlotFunc","LNAplot/PlotData","LNA/Krone","LNAutils/Pi")

local function g(x)
return
math.sin(6*x)+x^3
end

local function f(x)
return math.atan(g(math.tan(x)))
end

local function dfdx(x) return
(6*math.cos(6*math.tan(x))*(1/math.cos(x))^2+3*(1/math.cos(x))^2*math.tan(x)^2)/(1+(math.sin(6*math.tan(x))+math.tan(x)^3)^2)
end

local function d2fdx2(x) return
(-
18*(1/math.cos(x))^4*(2*math.cos(6*math.tan(x))+math.tan(x)^2)^2*(math.sin(6*math.tan(x))
+math.tan(x)^3)+6*(1/math.cos(x))^2*(2*math.cos(6*math.tan(x))*math.tan(x)+math.tan(x)^3
+(1/math.cos(x))^2*(-
6*math.sin(6*math.tan(x))+math.tan(x)))*(1+(math.sin(6*math.tan(x))+math.tan(x)^3)^2))/(1+(
math.sin(6*math.tan(x))+math.tan(x)^3)^2)^2
end

local Nr,roots,axesdata

roots,Nr=KroneRoots(f,dfdx,d2fdx2,-Pi/2,Pi/2)
print(Nr.." roots found:")
for i,v in ipairs(roots) do print(i,math.tan(v)) end
froots={}
for j=1,Nr do froots[j]=g(math.tan(roots[j])) end
print("\nFunction values at roots:")
for i,v in ipairs(froots) do print(i,v) end

axesdata=PlotFunc(f,{-Pi/2,Pi/2},{-Pi/2,Pi/2},false)
PlotData(roots,froots,{},axesdata,true,2)
```

Screen Capture Showing The Results:

Screen Capture Showing The Results Visually:

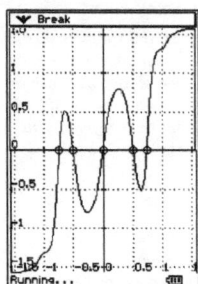

Checking The Results Using Mathematica:

Mathematica Code

```
FindRoot[Sin[6*x]+(x)^3==0,{x,{-.9,-.5,0,.5,.9}}]
```

Result:

```
{x→{-0.90689,-0.551723,0.,0.551723,0.90689}}
```

As you can see the results are true.

Requirements [2] :
Please note that the following documents (the requirement section) are Copyrighted by PAP [Developer oF the LNA (Lua Numerical Analysis) Package] .

KroneRoots
The function KroneRoots computes all the roots of a function within a given interval , or , optionally , a prescribed number of roots . It can be used locating and computing all roots of a function within a given interval .The algorithm implemented in this function is based on the Kronecher-Picard theory (hence its name) , and uses recursive auxiliary functions. It is currently the most complex algorithm included in LNA .Despite its complexity , however, the function can be easily called in a user program.

Syntax

> roots ,Nr=KroneRoots(f,dfdx,d2fdx2,a,b,r_reg,xi)

returns a vector roots , containing all the roots of the function f inside the interval {a,b}; optionally , it may return only a prescribed number of roots . This function also returns the total number of roots , Nr. The arguments dfdx, and d2fdx2 define the first and second derivatives of the function , respectively. The arguments r_reg controls how many roots should be returned. If omitted , or if r_reg<= 0 , all the roots will be returned . The optional argument xi defines an appropriate number , such that xi*dfdx(x) is not too small (or too large) compared to f(x) , for all x inside the interval {a,b} . The default value is xi=1.

Bisect
The function Bisect computes the root of a function within a given interval via the Bisection method .This is the simplest (and the slowest) method for root finding . However , its convergence is always guaranteed , and it is ofen used by more complex numerical methods . The algorithm implemented in Bisect is a modification of the "classic" algorithm , sometimes called "Simplified Bisection" , and it is slightly faster.

Syntax

> root,error=Bisect(f,xl,xr,eps,maxit,show)

returns the root of the function f inside the interval {xl,xr}, together with estimation of the absolute error . The arguments eps, maxit and show are optional. Eps defines the desired accuracy (default : Epsilon, i.e., 1.12×10^{-16}); it can be set to "auto", which is equivalent to the default accuracy. maxit defines the maximum number of iterations (default : 100) . show is a

Boolean argument that control wether progress of the iterative process will displayed or not (default : false); if set to true, the function value, $f(root)$, at each iteration will be displayed.

Romberg :

The function *Romberg* computes the definite integral of a function via the Romberg Method.

Syntax :

    q=Romberg(f,a,b,eps,k,show)

returns the definite integral, *q*, of the function f, integrated from *a* to *b*. The arguments *eps* , *k*, and show are optional : *eps* defines the desired accuracy . *k* defines the order of the method ; *show* is a Boolean argument that controls wether an integration progress will be displayed or not.

LNA Utility Constants And Functions :

Epsilon
The constant *Epsilon* defines the smallest positive number, ε, which satisfies inequality $1+\varepsilon > 1$. Due to computer arithmetic, adding a very small number to unity result *exactly* one. This constant defines *Epsilon* as $\varepsilon = 1.12810^{-16}$

Pi
The constant Pi defines π. Since π is often used in numerical computations, it is defined as a LNA constant, accurate to 16 digits. This constant defines Pi as $\pi = 3.1415927410125732$

Part
The function Part return part of a vector *A*, containing elements from *A[imin]* to *A[imax]*

Syntax

    P=Part(A,imin.imax)

Return a vector *P*, with imax-imin+1 elements, so that $P[1]=A[imin]$, $P[2]=A[imin+1]$, and so on, until $P[imax-imin+1]=A[imax]$

The codes required to run the driver program [2]

The Following codes are copyrighted by PAP [Developer of LNA (Lua Numerical Analysis) Package]

LNA/Krone

```
require("table","LNA/Bisect","LNA/Romberg")

local f,dfdx,d2fdx2
local roots
local xi=1
local nr,cr

local function KroneIntg(x)
local dfsq=dfdx(x)^2
return (f(x)*d2fdx2(x)-dfsq)/(f(x)^2+xi^2*dfsq)
end

local function Nroots(a,b)
local Nr
Nr=Romberg(KroneIntg,a,b,0.1)
Nr=-0.3183098861837907*(xi*Nr-math.atan(xi*dfdx(b)/f(b))+math.atan(xi*dfdx(a)/f(a)))
Nr=math.floor(Nr+0.49999999999999)
return Nr
end

local function Roots(a,b,Nr)
local subs,h,xl,xr,Njr
if Nr==1 then
 cr=cr+1
 roots[cr]=Bisect(f,a,b)
else
 subs=math.max(2,Nr)
 h=(b-a)/subs;xr=a
 for j=1,subs do
  xl,xr=xr,xr+h
  if j<subs then
   Njr=Nroots(xl,xr)
  else
   Njr=Nr-Njr
  end
  if Njr>0 then
```

```
   Roots(xl,xr,Njr)
    if cr==nr then
     return
    end
   end
  end
 end
end

function KroneRoots(g,dgdx,d2gdx2,a,b,...)
 f=g;dfdx=dgdx;d2fdx2=d2gdx2
 local Nr
 if a==b then
  print("Error: KroneRoots: Wrong inteval")
 elseif a>b then
  a,b=b,a
 end
 if arg["n"]>=2 then
  xi=arg[2]
 end
 Nr=Nroots(a,b)
 if Nr>0 then
  if arg["n"]>=1 then
   if arg[1]<=0 then
    nr=Nr
   elseif arg[1]<=Nr then
    nr=arg[1]
   else
    nr=Nr
    print("Warning: KroneRoots: Interval contains fewer roots than those required.")
   end
  else
   nr=Nr
  end
  roots={}
  cr=0
  Roots(a,b,Nr)
 else
  print("Warning: KroneRoots: No simple roots found.")
 end
 return roots,Nr
end

export{KroneRoots=KroneRoots}
LNA/Bisect
```

```
require("LNAutils/Epsilon")

function Bisect(f,xl,xr,...)
 local eps=Epsilon
 local maxit=100
 local show=false
 if arg["n"]>=1 then
  if arg[1]~="auto" then
  eps=arg[1] end
  if arg["n"]>=2 then
   maxit=arg[2]
   if arg["n"]>=3 then
    show=arg[3]
   end
  end
 end
 local root,error
 local xp,xc,fc,sl,sp,half
 xp=xl;xc=xl
 sl=math.sign(1,f(xl))
 sp=sl;half=xr-xl
 if sl*math.sign(1,f(xr))>0 then
  print("Error: Bisect: Interval does not contain a root, or contains an even number of roots.")
  return
 end
 if show then print(" i  discrepancy") end
 for i=1,maxit do
  half=0.5*half
  xc=xp+sl*sp*half
  fc=f(xc)
  if show then printf("%2i  %+e\n",i,fc) end
  if half<=eps then
   root=xc;error=half
   return root,error
  end
  if fc==0 then
   root=xc;error=0
   return root,error
  else
   xp=xc
   sp=math.sign(1,fc)
  end
 end
 root=xc;error=half
 print("Warning: Bisect: Iterations limit reached, but the accuracy is not satisfied.")
 return root,error
```

```
end

export{Bisect=Bisect}
```

LNAutils/Epsilon

```
Epsilon=1.12E-16
export{Epsilon=Epsilon}
```

LNA/Romberg

```
require("table","LNAutils/Part")

local function TrapStep(f,a,b,t,n)
local s
local it,del,x,su
if n==1 then
 s=0.5*(b-a)*(f(a)+f(b))
else
 it=2^(n-2);del=(b-a)/it
 x=a+0.5*del
 su=0
 for j=1,it do
  su=su+f(x);x=x+del
 end
 s=0.5*(t+(b-a)*su/it)
end
return s
end

local function PolIntrp(xa,ya,x)
local y,dy
local n=table.getn(xa)
local ns,dif,dift,c,d,ho
   ,hp,w,den
c=table.copy(ya)
d=table.copy(ya)
ns=1
dif=math.abs(x-xa[1])
for i=1,n do
 dift=math.abs(x-xa[i])
```

```
  if dift<dif then
   ns=i;dif=dift
  end
 end
 y=ya[ns];ns=ns-1
 for m=1,n-1 do
  for i=1,n-m do
   ho=xa[i]-x
   hp=xa[i+m]-x
   w=c[i+1]-d[i]
   den=ho-hp
   if den==0 then
    print("Error: Romberg: Roundoff error.")
    return
   end
   den=w/den
   d[i]=hp*den
   c[i]=ho*den
  end
  if 2*ns<n-m then
   dy=c[ns+1]
  else
   dy=d[ns];ns=ns-1
  end
  y=y+dy
 end
 return y,dy
end

local function Reached(q,dq,eps)
 local ok
 if eps>0 then
  ok=math.abs(dq)<eps
 else
  ok=math.abs(dq)<
    -eps*math.abs(q)
 end
 return ok
end

function Romberg(f,a,b,...)
 local q
 local eps=1E-6
 local k=2
 local show=false
 local km,dq,h,s
```

```
local jmax=20
local jmaxp=jmax+1
if arg["n"]>=1 then
 eps=arg[1]
 if arg["n"]>=2 then
  k=arg[2]
  if arg["n"]>=3 then
   show=arg[3]
  end
 end
end
km=k-1
h={};s={}
h[1]=1
for j=1,jmax do
 s[j]=TrapStep(f,a,b,s[j],j)
 if j>=k then
  q,dq=PolIntrp(Part(h,j-km,j),Part(s,j-km,j),0)
  if show then print(j,q)
  end
  if Reached(q,dq,eps) then
   return q
  end
 end
 s[j+1]=s[j]
 h[j+1]=0.25*h[j]
end
print("Warning: Romberg: Maximum number of iterations reached, but the acuracy criterion is not satisfied.")
return q
end

export{Romberg=Romberg}
```

LNAutils/Part

```
function Part(A,imin,imax)
local P
P={}
for i=imin,imax do
 P[i-imin+1]=A[i]
end
return P
```

```
end
```

```
export{Part=Part}
```

PlotFunc

```
require ("table","draw","LNAplot/PlotUtil")

function PlotFunc(f,xv,yv,...)
--Optional arguments:
local wait=true
local lwidth={1}
local tics={"auto","auto"}
local grid=true
local lblpos={0,0}
local lblsize={9,9}
local c="auto"
local discont={}
--
local scale
local lws,funcs,x,xp,X,Xp,Y,Yp,disconts
local id={}
if arg["n"]>=1 then
 wait=arg[1]
 if arg["n"]>=2 then
  lwidth=arg[2]
  if type(lwidth)=="number" then
   lwidth={lwidth}
  end
  if arg["n"]>=3 then
   tics=arg[3]
   if type(tics)~="table" then
    tics={tics,tics}
   end
   if arg["n"]>=4 then
    grid=arg[4]
    if arg["n"]>=5 then
     lblpos=arg[5]
     if type(lblpos)=="number" then
      lblpos={lblpos,lblpos}
     end
     if arg["n"]>=6 then
      lblsize=arg[6]
```

```
    if type(lblsize)=="number" then
     lblsize={lblsize,lblsize}
    end
    if arg["n"]>=7 then
     c=arg[7]
     if arg["n"]>=8 then
      discont=arg[8]
     end
    end
   end
  end
 end
end
end
lws=#lwidth
if type(f)=="function" then
 f={f}
end
funcs=#f
for i=lws+1,funcs do
 lwidth[i]=lwidth[lws]
end
discont,disconts=Discontinuities(funcs,discont)
for i=1,funcs do
 id[i]=1
 table.sort(discont[i])
end
draw.onbuffer()
if xv[1]~=nil then
 scale=SetScale(xv,yv)
 PlotAxes(xv,yv,scale,tics,grid,lblpos,lblsize,c)
else
 xv=yv[1]
 scale=yv[3]
 yv=yv[2]
end
Xp=0;xp=xv[1]
Y={};Yp={}
for i=1,funcs do
 Yp[i]=(yv[2]-f[i](xv[1]))*scale[2]
end
for X=1,X_pixels do
 x=xv[1]+X/scale[1]
 for i=1,funcs do
  Y[i]=(yv[2]-f[i](x))*scale[2]
```

```
  if id[i]>disconts[i] or x<discont[i][id[i]] or xp>discont[i][id[i]] then
   draw.line(Xp,Yp[i],X,Y[i],1,lwidth[i])
   elseif xp<=discont[i][id[i]] and x>=discont[i][id[i]] then
    id[i]=id[i]+1
   end
   Yp[i]=Y[i]
  end
 xp=x;Xp=X
end
showgraph()
draw.update()
if wait then waitkey() end
showconsole()
return {xv,yv,scale}
end

export{PlotFunc=PlotFunc}
```

LNAplot/PlotUtil

```
require ("string","table","draw","LNAutils/OrderMag")

X_max=158
Y_max=213
X_center=79
Y_center=106
X_pixels=159
Y_pixels=214

local function SetScale(xv,yv)
local xscale,yscale
xscale=X_pixels/(xv[2]-xv[1])
yscale=Y_pixels/(yv[2]-yv[1])
return {xscale,yscale}
end

local function AutoXtics(range)
--tics=math.max(math.floor(range/7),1)
local tics=OrderMag(range)
if range<4*tics then
 tics=tics/2
end
return tics
```

```
end

local function AutoYtics(range)
--tics=math.max(math.floor((yv[2]-yv[1])/9),1)
local tics=OrderMag(range)
if range<4*tics then
 tics=tics/2
end
return tics
end

function Discontinuities(funcs,discont)
local D=table.copy(discont)
local id={}
local disconts={}
for i=1,funcs do
 if D[i]==nil then
  D[i]={}
 elseif type(D[i])=="number" then
  D[i]={D[i]}
 end
 disconts[i]=#D[i]
end
return D,disconts
end

function PlotAxes(xv,yv,scale,tics,grid,lblpos,lblsize,c)
local Xc,Yc,X,Y,Xl,Yl,lblxp,lblyp
local lblcut=1E-8
--Auto tics selection:
if tics[1]=="auto" then
 tics[1]=AutoXtics(xv[2]-xv[1])
end
if tics[2]=="auto" then
 tics[2]=AutoYtics(yv[2]-yv[1])
end
--
if c=="auto" then
 c={0,0}
end
--[[ AXES ]]--
Xc=(c[1]-xv[1])*scale[1]
Yc=(yv[2]-c[2])*scale[2]
draw.line(0,Yc,X_max,Yc)
draw.line(Xc,0,Xc,Y_max)
--[[ TICS & GRID ]]--
```

```
if lblpos[1]==0 then
 Yl=Y_pixels-lblsize[1]
else
 Yl=Yc+1
end
if lblpos[2]==0 then
 Xl=2
else
 Xl=Xc+2
end
for xp=c[1]-math.floor((c[1]-xv[1])/tics[1])*tics[1],math.floor((xv[2]-c[1])/tics[1])*tics[1],tics[1] do
 X=(xp-xv[1])*scale[1]
 draw.line(X,Yc-2,X,Yc+2)
 if grid then
  for Y=0,Y_pixels,4 do
   draw.pixel(X,Y)
  end
 end
 if lblsize[1]>0 and X>0 and X<X_pixels then
  lblxp=xp
  if math.abs(xp)<=lblcut then
   lblxp=0
  end
  draw.text(X+2,Yl,lblxp,1,lblsize[1])
 end
end
for yp=c[2]-math.floor((c[2]-yv[1])/tics[2])*tics[2],math.floor((yv[2]-c[2])/tics[2])*tics[2],tics[2] do
 Y=(yv[2]-yp)*scale[2]
 draw.line(Xc-2,Y,Xc+2,Y)
 if grid then
  for X=0,X_pixels,4 do
   draw.pixel(X,Y)
  end
 end
 if lblsize[2]>0 and Y>0 and Y<Y_pixels then
  lblyp=yp
  if math.abs(yp)<=lblcut then
   lblyp=0
  end
  draw.text(Xl,Y-lblsize[2],lblyp,1,lblsize[2])
 end
end
end
```

```
function PlotPoint(X,Y,pointtype,pointsize)
--Non-filled circle:
if pointtype==0 then
 draw.point(X,Y,1,pointsize)
elseif pointtype==1 then
 draw.circle(X,Y,pointsize,1,1,-1)
 draw.point(X,Y)
--Crossed circle:
elseif pointtype==2 then
 draw.circle(X,Y,pointsize,1,1,-1)
 draw.line(X-pointsize,Y,X+pointsize,Y)
 draw.line(X,Y-pointsize,X,Y+pointsize)
--Filled circle:
elseif pointtype==3 then
 draw.circle(X,Y,pointsize,1,1,1)
--Non-filled rectangle:
elseif pointtype==4 then
 draw.rect(X-pointsize,Y-pointsize,X+pointsize,Y+pointsize,1,1,-1)
 draw.point(X,Y)
--Crossed rectangle:
elseif pointtype==5 then
 draw.rect(X-pointsize,Y-pointsize,X+pointsize,Y+pointsize,1,1,-1)
 draw.line(X-pointsize,Y,X+pointsize,Y)
 draw.line(X,Y-pointsize,X,Y+pointsize)
--Filled rectangle:
elseif pointtype==6 then
 draw.rect(X-pointsize,Y-pointsize,X+pointsize,Y+pointsize,1,1,1)
end
end

local function DrawLabel()
return
end

export{X_max=X_max,Y_max=Y_max,X_center=X_center,Y_center=Y_center,X_pixels=X_pixels,Y_pixels=Y_pixels,SetScale=SetScale,Discontinuities=Discontinuities,PlotAxes=PlotAxes,PlotPoint=PlotPoint}
```

LNAutils/OrderMag

```
require("string")

function OrderMag(x)
```

```
local xexp=string.lower(string.format("%e",x))
local e=string.find(xexp,"e")
local n=string.len(xexp)
return 10^string.sub(xexp,e+1,n)
end

export{OrderMag=OrderMag}
```

LNAplot/PlotData

```
require ("table","draw","LNAplot/PlotUtil")

function PlotData(x,y,xv,yv,...)
--Optional arguments:
local wait=true
local ptype={1}
local psize={3}
local lwidth={0}
local tics={"auto","auto"}
local grid=true
local lblpos={0,0}
local lblsize={9,9}
local c="auto"
--
local points=#x
local scale
local sets,pws,lws,X,Xp,Y,Yp
if arg["n"]>=1 then
 wait=arg[1]
 if arg["n"]>=2 then
  ptype=arg[2]
  if type(ptype)=="number" then
   ptype={ptype}
  end
  if arg["n"]>=3 then
   psize=arg[3]
   if type(psize)=="number" then
    psize={psize}
   end
   if arg["n"]>=4 then
    lwidth=arg[4]
    if type(lwidth)=="number" then
     lwidth={lwidth}
```

```
    end
    if arg["n"]>=5 then
     tics=arg[5]
     if type(tics)~="table" then
      tics={tics,tics}
     end
     if arg["n"]>=6 then
      grid=arg[6]
      if arg["n"]>=7 then
       lblpos=arg[7]
       if type(lblpos)=="number" then
        lblpos={lblpos,lblpos}
       end
       if arg["n"]>=8 then
        lblsize=arg[8]
        if type(iblsize)=="number" then
         lblsize={lblsize,lblsize}
        end
        if arg["n"]>=9 then
         c=arg[9]
        end
       end
      end
     end
    end
   end
  end
 end
end
if type(y[1])=="number" then y={y} end
sets=#y
pws=#ptype
for i=pws+1,sets do
 ptype[i]=ptype[pws]
end
pws=#psize
for i=pws+1,sets do
 psize[i]=psize[pws]
end
lws=#lwidth
for i=lws+1,sets do
 lwidth[i]=lwidth[lws]
end
draw.onbuffer()
if xv[1]~=nil then
 scale=SetScale(xv,yv)
```

```
 PlotAxes(xv,yv,scale,tics,grid,lblpos,lblsize,c)
else
 xv=yv[1]
 scale=yv[3]
 yv=yv[2]
 end
Xp=(x[1]-xv[1])*scale[1]
Y={};Yp={}
for j=1,sets do
 Yp[j]=(yv[2]-y[j][1])*scale[2]
 PlotPoint(Xp,Yp[j],ptype[j],psize[j])
end
for i=2,points do
 X=(x[i]-xv[1])*scale[1]
 for j=1,sets do
  Y[j]=(yv[2]-y[j][i])*scale[2]
  if psize[j]>0 then
   PlotPoint(X,Y[j],ptype[j],psize[j])
  end
  if lwidth[j]>0 then
   draw.line(Xp,Yp[j],X,Y[j],1,lwidth[j])
   Yp[j]=Y[j]
  end
 end
 Xp=X
end
showgraph()
draw.update()
if wait then waitkey() end
showconsole()
return {xv,yv,scale}
end

export{PlotData=PlotData}
```

LNAutils/Pi

```
Pi=3.1415927410125732
export{Pi=Pi}
```

- **Developing A Method To Find The Finite Number Of Infinities Of The Functions.**

*T*o visually find the finite number of Infinities of the functions, first we should Infinity plot the function, then we should guess the Infinities using the Infinity Plot. Then we will use the Mathematica FindRoot Command to find the Infinities through the Transformed function. We will introduce the method through examples.

Example 1:
Find the Infinites of the following function:

$$f = \frac{5}{x^2 - 5}$$

Solution:
The Transformed function in Mathematica code will be:

$$\text{ArcTan}[\frac{5}{-5 + \text{Tan}[x]^2}]$$

The Infinity plot will be:

$$\text{Plot}[\text{ArcTan}[\frac{5}{-5 + \text{Tan}[x]^2}], \{x, -\frac{\pi}{2}, \frac{\pi}{2}\}]$$

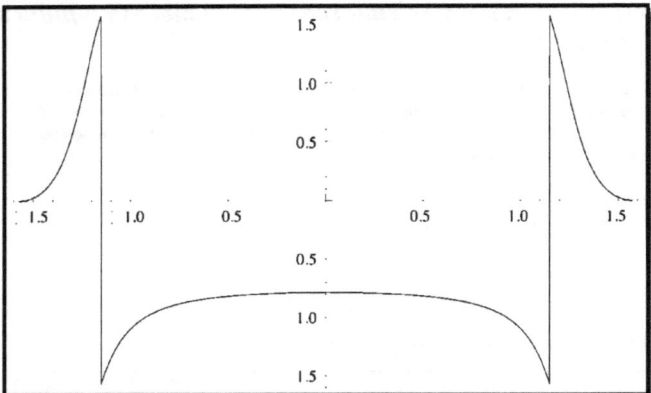

Using the plot we can guess the Infinities . +∞ (Positive Infinities) of the function can be find with the Initial guesses of {−1.16,1.16} through the transformed function .

The Mathematica code to find the Positive Infinities of the transformed function is as follows :

$$\text{FindRoot}[-\frac{\pi}{2} + \text{ArcTan}[\frac{5}{-5 + \text{Tan}[x]^2}], \{x, \{-1.16, 1.16\}\}]$$

Result :

```
{x -> {-1.1502619915113772`, 1.1502619915109316`}}
```

The Positive Infinities of the main function will be find using the following method (tangent of the results):

```
Tan[{-1.1502619915113772`, 1.1502619915109316`}]
```

Result :

```
{-2.236067977502464, 2.2360679774997902}
```

−∞ (Negative Infinities) of the function can be find with the Initial guesses of {−1.15,1.15} through the transformed function .

The Mathematica code to find the Negative Infinities of the transformed function is as follows :

$$\text{FindRoot}[+\frac{\pi}{2} + \text{ArcTan}[\frac{5}{-5 + \text{Tan}[x]^2}], \{x, \{-1.15, 1.15\}\}, \text{AccuracyGoal} \rightarrow 7]$$

Result :

$$\{x \rightarrow \{-1.1502619845593214`, 1.1502619753619217`\}\}$$

The Negative Infinities of the main function will be find using the following method (tangent of the results):

$$\text{Tan}[\{-1.1502619845593214`, 1.1502619753619217`\}]$$

Result :

$$\{-2.2360679357901296, 2.2360678806057344\}$$

Testing the results :

To test the results we will use the general methods of finding the asymptotes of the functions . The vertical Asymptote of the function will be find through the roots of the denominator of the function .

Vertical Asymptotes :

The Mathematica code to find the vertical Asymptotes is as follows :

$$N[\text{Solve}[x^2 - 5 == 0, x]]$$

Result :

$$\{\{x \rightarrow -2.23606797749979`\}, \{x \rightarrow 2.23606797749979`\}\}$$

You can see that the results are true .

Example 2 :

Find the Infinites of the following function :

$$f = \frac{5}{(x-1) \times (x+3) \times (x-6)}$$

Solution :
The Transformed function in Mathematica code will be :

$$\text{ArcTan}\left[\frac{5}{(-6 + \text{Tan}[x])(-1 + \text{Tan}[x])(3 + \text{Tan}[x])}\right]$$

The Infinity plot will be :

$$\text{Plot}\left[\text{ArcTan}\left[\frac{5}{(-6 + \text{Tan}[x])(-1 + \text{Tan}[x])(3 + \text{Tan}[x])}\right], \{x, -\frac{\pi}{2}, \frac{\pi}{2}\}, \text{PlotRange} \to \text{All}\right]$$

The Result will be as follows :

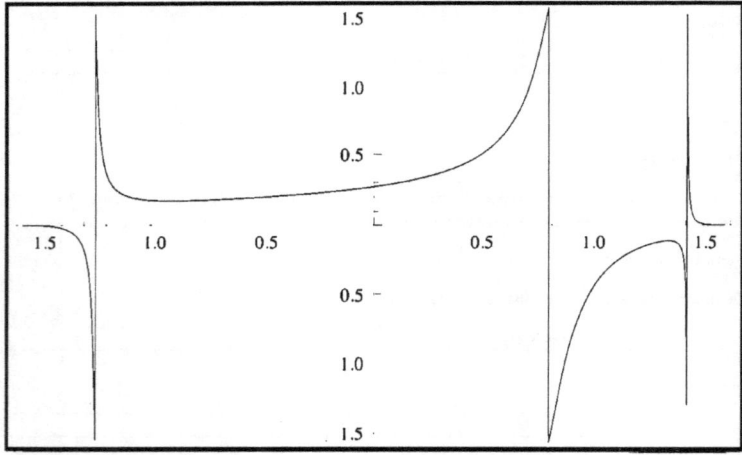

Using the plot we can guess the Infinities . $+\infty$ (Positive Infinities) of the function can be find with the Initial guesses of $\{-1.2, 0.75, 1.42\}$ through the transformed function .

The Mathematica code to find the Positive Infinities of the transformed function is as follows :

```
FindRoot[-π/2
+ ArcTan[5/((-6 + Tan[x])(-1 + Tan[x])(3 + Tan[x]))], {x, {-1.2, 0.75, 1.42}}, MaxIterations
→ 150, AccuracyGoal → 6]
```

Result :

```
{x -> {-1.2490457631598328`, 0.7853981415952962`, 1.4056476515052179`}}
```

The Positive Infinities of the main function will be find using the following method (tangent of the results):

```
Tan[{-1.2490457631598328`, 0.7853981415952962`, 1.4056476515052179`}]
```

Result :

```
{-3., 1., 6.}
```

or the result with 15 digits after the point will be :

```
{-2.999999907615787`, 0.999999956395€967`, 6.0000000786230805`}
```

−∞ (Negative Infinities) of the function can be find with the Initial guesses of {−1.3, 0.81, 1.39} through the transformed function .

The Mathematica code to find the Negative Infinities of the transformed function is as follows :

```
FindRoot[+π/2
+ ArcTan[5/((-6 + Tan[x])(-1 + Tan[x])(3 + Tan[x]))], {x, {-1.3, 0.81, 1.39}}, AccuracyGoal
→ 4]
```

Result :

```
{x -> {-1.2490468690695897`, 0.7854009174907848`, 1.4056475158794814`}}
```

The Negative Infinities of the main function will be find using the following method (tangent of the results):

```
Tan[{-1.2490468690695897`, 0.7854009174907848`, 1.4056475158794814`}]
```

Result :

> {−3.00001,1.00001,6.}

or the result with 15 digits after the point will be :

> {−3.000010966749434,1.000005508201843,5.999995060474788}

Testing the results :

To test the results we will use the general methods of finding the asymptotes of the functions . The vertical Asymptote of the function will be find through the roots of the denominator of the function .

Vertical Asymptotes :

The Mathematica code to find the vertical Asymptotes is as follows :

> $N[Solve[(x-1)*(x+3)*(x-6) == 0, x]]$

Result :

> $\{\{x \to -3.\}, \{x \to 1.\}, \{x \to 6.\}\}$

You can see that the results are true .

Example 3 :

Find the Infinites of the following function :

$$f = \frac{5}{\sin[6*(x^3 - 0.4)] + x^4}$$

Solution :

The Transformed function in Mathematica code will be :

> $ArcTan[\dfrac{5}{\sin[6*(Tan[x])^3 - 0.4)] + Tan[x]^4}]$

The Infinity plot will be :

> $Plot[ArcTan[\dfrac{5}{\sin[6(-0.4 + Tan[x]^3)] + Tan[x]^4}], \{x, -\dfrac{\pi}{2}, \dfrac{\pi}{2}\}, PlotRange \to \{-\dfrac{\pi}{2}, \dfrac{\pi}{2}\}]$

The Result will be as follows :

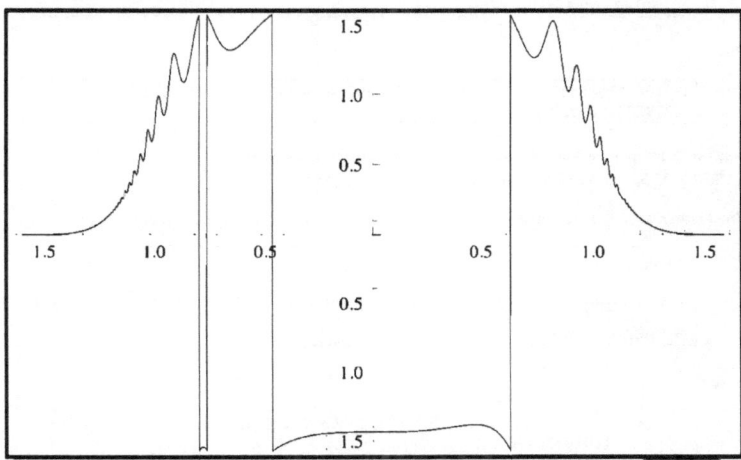

Using the plot we can guess the Infinities. +∞ (Positive Infinities) of the function can be find with the Initial guesses of {−0.8, −0.73, −0.48, 0.63} through the transformed function.

The Mathematica code to find the Positive Infinities of the transformed function is as follows :

```
FindRoot[-π/2
+ ArcTan[5/(Sin[6(-0.4 + Tan[x]³)] + Tan[x]⁴)], {x, {-0.8, -0.73, -0.48, 0.63}}, MaxIterations
→ 150]
```

Result :

{x → {−0.7789523837360715, −0.7442419437453658, −0.4518738358393392, 0.6171284554985426}}

The Positive Infinities of the main function will be find using the following method (tangent of the results):

Tan[{−0.7789523837360715, −0.7442419437453658, −0.4518738358393392, 0.6171284554985426}]

Result :

{−0.9871908283758791, −0.9208984161497941, −0.48536824294300907, 0.7095827903029706}

−∞ (Negative Infinities) of the function can be find with the Initial guesses of {−0.77, −0.75, −0.44, 0.6} through the transformed function .

The Mathematica code to find the Negative Infinities of the transformed function is as follows :

FindRoot[$+\frac{\pi}{2}$ + ArcTan[$\frac{5}{\text{Sin}[6(-0.4 + \text{Tan}[x]^3)] + \text{Tan}[x]^4}$], {x, {−0.77, −0.75, −0.44, 0.6}}, MaxIterations → 150, AccuracyGoal → 6]

Result :

{x → {−0.7789522798492675, −0.7442420311869101, −0.45187363699060945, 0.6171281837619244}}

The Negative Infinities of the main function will be find using the following method (tangent of the results):

Tan[{−0.7789522798492675, −0.7442420311869101, −0.45187363699060945, 0.6171281837619244}]

Result :

{−0.9871906232466549, −0.9208985777464935, −0.4853679972490557, 0.7095823817449417}

Testing the results :

To test the results we will use the general methods of finding the asymptotes of the functions . The vertical Asymptote of the function will be find through the roots of the denominator of the function .

Vertical Asymptotes :

The Mathematica code to find the vertical Asymptotes is as follows :

FindRoot[Sin[6 * $(x^3 - 0.4)$]
+ x^4, {x, {−0.9871908283758791, −0.9208984161497941, −0.48536824294300907, 0.7095827903029706}}]

Result :

{x → {−0.9871908283758782, −0.9208984161497942, −0.48536824193310446, 0.7095827903029706}}

You can see that the results are true .

Lua Driver Program to find the Vertical Asymptotes are as follows :
We should break the Domain to 3 domains . The Domains are :

$$-\frac{\pi}{2} < x < 1 \quad , \quad -1 < z < 1 \quad , \quad 1 < x < \frac{\pi}{2}$$

```
require("LNAplot/PlotFunc","LNAplot/PlotData","LNA/Krone","LNAutils/Pi")

local function g(x)
return
math.sin(6*(x^3-0.4))+x^4
end

local function f(x)
return
math.atan(math.sin(6*(-0.4+(math.tan(x))^3))+(math.tan(x))^4)
end

local function dfdx(x) return
(18*math.cos(6*(-
0.4+(math.tan(x))^3))*(1/math.cos(x))^2*(math.tan(x))^2+4*(1/math.cos(x))^2*(math.tan(x))^3
)/(1+(math.sin(6*(-0.4+(math.tan(x))^3))+(math.tan(x))^4)^2)
end

local function d2fdx2(x)
return
-((2*(18*math.cos(6*(-
0.4+(math.tan(x))^3))*(1/math.cos(x))^2*(math.tan(x))^2+4*(1/math.cos(x))^2*(math.tan(x))^3
)^2*(math.sin(6*(-0.4+(math.tan(x))^3))+(math.tan(x))^4))/(1+(math.sin(6*(-
0.4+(math.tan(x))^3))+(math.tan(x))^4)^2)^2)+(36*math.cos(6*(-
0.4+(math.tan(x))^3))*(1/math.cos(x))^4*math.tan(x)+12*(1/math.cos(x))^4*(math.tan(x))^2+3
6*math.cos(6*(-
0.4+(math.tan(x))^3))*(1/math.cos(x))^2*(math.tan(x))^3+8*(1/math.cos(x))^2*(math.tan(x))^4
```

```
-324*(1/math.cos(x))^4*math.sin(6*(-0.4+(math.tan(x))^3))*(math.tan(x))^4)/(1+(math.sin(6*(-
0.4+(math.tan(x))^3))+(math.tan(x))^4)^2)
end

local Nr,roots,axesdata

roots,Nr=KroneRoots(f,dfdx,d2fdx2,-1,1)
print(Nr.." roots found:")
if Nr~=0 then
for i,v in ipairs(roots) do print(i,math.tan(v)) end
froots={}
for j=1,Nr do froots[j]=g(math.tan(roots[j])) end
print("\nFunction values at roots:")
for i,v in ipairs(froots) do print(i,v) end

axesdata=PlotFunc(f,{-Pi/2,Pi/2},{-Pi/2,Pi/2},false)
PlotData(roots,froots,{},axesdata,true,2)
end
```

The Output for the specified domains will be as follow :

$-\frac{\pi}{2} < x < 1$ $-1 < x < 1$ $1 < x < \frac{\pi}{2}$

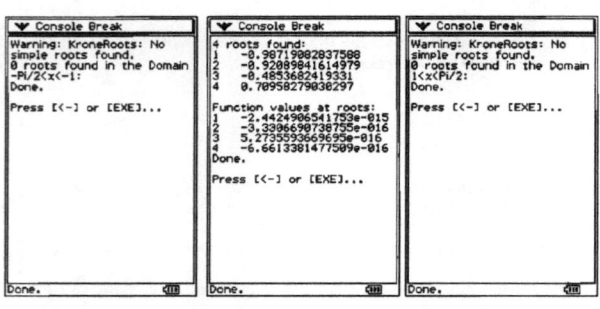

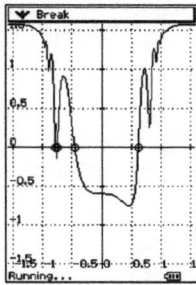

Example 4 :

Find the Infinites of the following function :

$f = \tan(2 \times x) + x^3$

Solution :
The Transformed function in Mathematica code will be :

$$ArcTan[Tan[2 * Tan[x]] + Tan[x]^3]$$

The Infinity plot will be :

$$Plot[ArcTan[Tan[2 * Tan[x]] + Tan[x]^3], \{x, -\frac{\pi}{2}, \frac{\pi}{2}\}, PlotRange \rightarrow All]$$

The Result will be as follows :

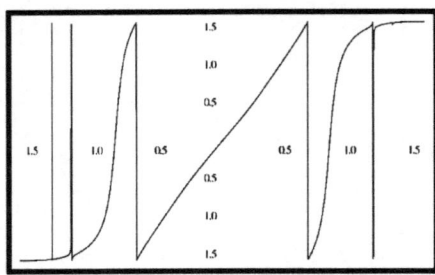

Using the plot we can guess the Infinities. +∞ (Positive Infinities) of the function can be find with the Initial guesses of {−1.3216, −1.17, −0.7,0.6,1} through the transformed function.

The Mathematica code to find the Positive Infinities of the transformed function is as follows :

```
FindRoot[−π/2 + ArcTan[Tan[2 * Tan[x]]
        + Tan[x]^3], {x, {−1.3216, −1.17, −0.7,0.6,1,1.3}}, MaxIterations
        → 1000, AccuracyGoal → 6]
```

Result :

{x → {−1.321447987003392, −1.169422842065824, −0.6657737930180916, 0.6657736844488363,1.1694228046197082,1.3214479485830937}}

The Positive Infinities of the main function will be find using the following method (tangent of the results):

Tan[{−1.321447987003392, −1.169422842065824, −0.6657737930180916, 0.6657736844488363,1.1694228046197082,1.3214479485830937}]

Result :

{−3.926991132598397, −2.3561946032087975, −0.7853982329054199, 0.7853980573651929,2.356194357874862,3.9269905016888096}

−∞ (Negative Infinities) of the function can be find with the Initial guesses of
{−1.32, −1.165, −.6,0.7,1.17,1.322} through the transformed function.

The Mathematica code to find the Negative Infinities of the transformed function is as follows :

```
FindRoot[π/2 + ArcTan[Tan[2 * Tan[x]]
        + Tan[x]^3], {x, {-1.32, -1.165, -.6, 0.7, 1.17, 1.322}}, MaxIterations → 300]
```

Result :

```
{x → {-1.3214479677754711, -1.1694228247122458, -0.6657737474122314,
0.6657737517571516, 1.169422824845148, 1.3214479678320301}}
```

The Negative Infinities of the main function will be find using the following method (tangent of the results):

```
Tan[{-1.3214479677754711, -1.1694228247122458, -0.6657737474122314,
0.6657737517571516, 1.169422824845148, 1.3214479678320301}]
```

Result :

```
{-3.9269908168517462, -2.3561944895141798, -0.7853981591675699,
0.7853981661926553, 2.356194490384908, 3.3269908177805157}
```

Now we want to go further and find the infinities that are not visible on the distorted plot with the domain of $[-\frac{\pi}{2}, \frac{\pi}{2}]$. To find the invisible asymptotes we should use shorter domains for the infinity plot. We just show one example of invisible asymptote, So we plot the transformed function in a shorter domain as follow :

```
Plot[ArcTan[Tan[2 * Tan[x]] + Tan[x]^3], {x, -1.391, -1.3908}, PlotRange → All]
```
Result :

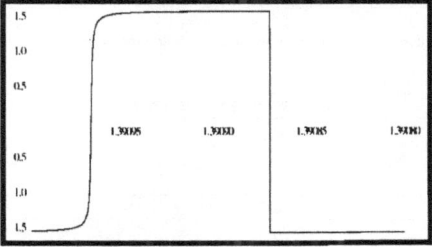

+∞ (Positive Infinities) of the function can be find with the Initial guesses of {−1.3909} through the transformed function.
The Mathematica code to find the Positive Infinitiy of the transformed function is as follows :

```
FindRoot[−π/2 + ArcTan[Tan[2 ∗ Tan[x]] + Tan[x]^3], {x, −1.3909}, MaxIterations
    → 1000, AccuracyGoal → 6]
```

The Result is :

```
{x → −1.3908719929660696}
```

The Positive Infinitiy of the main function will be find using the following method (tangent of the results):

```
Tan[−1.3908719929660696]
```

The Result :

```
                    −5.49778729840062
```

−∞ (Negative Infinities) of the function can be find with the Initial guesses of {−1.3909} through the transformed function.
The Mathematica code to find the Negative Infinitiy of the transformed function is as follows :

```
FindRoot[+π/2 + ArcTan[Tan[2 ∗ Tan[x]] + Tan[x]^3], {x, −1.3985}, MaxIterations
    → 1000, AccuracyGoal → 6]
```

The Result is :

```
x → −1.390871972974362}
```

The Positive Infinitiy of the main function will be find using the following method (tangent of the results):

```
Tan[−1.390871972974362]
```

The Result :

```
                    −5.49778667414632
```

- **Developing A Method To Find The Absolute Maximum And Minimum Of Functions In The Domain $(-\infty, +\infty)$.**

To find the Absolute maximum and minimum of functions in the domain $(-\infty, +\infty)$ we can use the ArcTan transformation and find the Absolute maximum and minimum of the transformed function in the domain $\left[-\frac{\pi}{2}, +\frac{\pi}{2}\right]$.

We introduce the method by some examples :

Example 1:

Find the Absolute Maximum and Minimum of the following function :

$f(x) = x^2$

The Maple Code to define the function and its transformed mode is as follows :

$f1 := x \to x^2$

$$x \to x^2$$

$f2 := x \to \arctan(f1(\tan(x)))$

$$x \to \arctan(f1(\tan(x)))$$

The Maple code to calculate the Maximum of the transformed function is as follows :

$$\text{maximize}\left(f2(x), x = -\frac{\pi}{2} .. \frac{\pi}{2}, \text{location}\right)$$

$$\frac{1}{2}\pi, \left\{\left[\left\{x = -\frac{1}{2}\pi\right\}, \frac{1}{2}\pi\right], \left[\left\{x = \frac{1}{2}\pi\right\}, \frac{1}{2}\pi\right]\right\}$$

The Mathematica code to calculate the Absolute Maximum of the main function is as follows :

```
Tan[π/2]
```

The result is :

```
ComplexInfinity
```

The Maple code to check the result is as follows :

$$\mathit{maximize}(f1(x), \mathit{location})$$

$$\infty, \{[\{x = \infty\}, \infty], [\{x = -\infty\}, \infty]\}$$

As you Can see the result is true .

Now we Calculate the absolute minimum :

The Maple code to calculate the Minimum of the transformed function is as follows :

$$\mathit{minimize}\left(f2(x), x = -\frac{\pi}{2} .. \frac{\pi}{2}, \mathit{location}\right)$$

$$0, \{[\{x = 0\}, 0]\}$$

The Maple code to calculate the Absolute minimum of the main function is as follows :

$$\tan(0)$$

$$0$$

The Maple code to check the result is as follows :

$$\mathit{minimize}(f1(x), \mathit{location})$$

$$0, \{[\{x = 0\}, 0]\}$$

As you can see the result is true .

Example 2 :

Find the Absolute minimum and maximum of the following function :

$$f(x) = \left|e^{-x^2} - \frac{1}{2}\right|$$

The Maple Code to define the function and its transformed mode is as follows :

$$f1 := x \to \left|e^{-x^2} - \frac{1}{2}\right|$$

$$x \to \left|e^{-x^2} - \frac{1}{2}\right|$$

$$f2 := x \to \arctan(f1(\tan(x)))$$

$$x \to \arctan(f1(\tan(x)))$$

The Maple code to calculate the Maximum of the transformed function is as follows :

$$maximize\left(f2(x), x = -\frac{\pi}{2} .. \frac{\pi}{2}, location\right)$$

$$\arctan\left(\frac{1}{2}\right), \left\{\left[\{x = 0\}, \arctan\left(\frac{1}{2}\right)\right]\right\}$$

The Maple code to calculate the Absolute Maximum of the main function is as follows :

$$\tan\left(\arctan\left(\frac{1}{2}\right)\right)$$

$$\frac{1}{2}$$

The Maple code to check the result is as follows :

$$maximize(f1(x), location)$$

$$\frac{1}{2}, \left\{\left[\{x = 0\}, \frac{1}{2}\right]\right\}$$

As you Can see the result is true .

Now we Calculate the absolute minimum :

The Maple code to calculate the Minimum of the transformed function is as follows :

$$minimize\left(f2(x), x = -\frac{\pi}{2} .. \frac{\pi}{2}, location\right)$$

$$0, \left\{\left[\{x = -\arctan(\sqrt{\ln(2)})\}, 0\right], \left[\{x = \arctan(\sqrt{\ln(2)})\}, 0\right]\right\}$$

The Maple code to calculate the Absolute minimum of the main function is as follows :

$$\tan(0)$$

$$0$$

The Maple code to check the result is as follows :

$$minimize(f1(x), location)$$

$$0, \left\{\left[\{x = \sqrt{\ln(2)}\}, 0\right], \left[\{x = -\sqrt{\ln(2)}\}, 0\right]\right\}$$

As you can see the result is true .

ANALITYCAL METHOD

Now after seeing the applications of Infinity Plots, we will develop an Analytical method to find the unsolved limits of mentioned functions at the introduction of the article.

The method is as follows :

We will use the transformed function using the following transformation :

$$ArcTan\left(f(Tan(x))\right) \qquad D_f = \left[-\frac{\pi}{2}, \frac{\pi}{2}\right] \ , \ R_f = \left[-\frac{\pi}{2}, \frac{\pi}{2}\right]$$

And we can use $x \to (\frac{\pi}{2} - \$MachineEpsilon)$ instead of the $x \to +\infty$ in the transformed function.

So the limit will be changed to

$$\lim_{x \to (\frac{\pi}{2} - \$MachineEpsilon)} [ArcTan\left(f(Tan(x))\right)]$$

Where f is the defined function :

f=Function [{x},Intg[x]/x]

So the Mathematica Code to Solve the Limit will be as follows :

```
Intg=Function[{x}, If[IntegerPart[x]≥0,IntegerPart[x],IntegerPart[x]-1]];
F2= Function[{x},ArcTan[F1[Tan[x]]]];
Y=F2[π/2 − $MachineEpsilon];
Tan[Y]
```

Output :

1

So you can see that the Analytical method and the graphical method yield the same result.

Further Examples :

3D INFINITY PLOTS

*I*t is possible to develop 3D Infinity Plots. The technique is the same as the 2D Infinity Plots.
Here is some examples :

```
F= Function[{x,y},{x^2+y^2,-x^2-y^2}];
Plot3D[ArcTan[F [Tan[x],Tan[y]]],{x,-π/2, π /2},{y,-π /2, π /2},ColorFunction→"RustTones"]
```

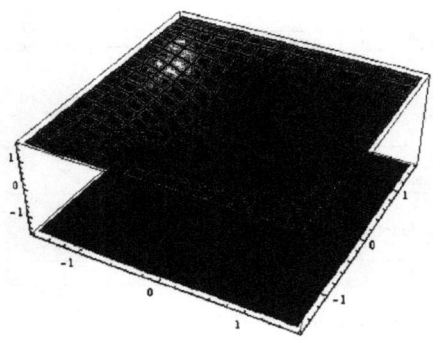

```
F= Function[{x,y},{x^2-y^2}]
Plot3D[ArcTan[F [Tan[x],Tan[y]]],{x,- π /2, π /2},{y,- π /2, π
/2},RegionFunction→Function[{x,y,z},2<x^2+y^2<9],BoxRatios→Automatic]
```

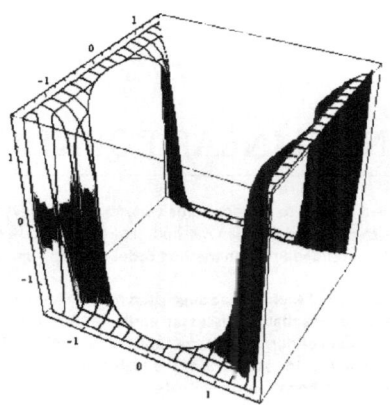

```
F= Function[{x,y},x^2-y^2]
F5Region= Function[{x,y,z},2<x^2+y^2<9]
ContourPlot[ArcTan[F5[Tan[x],Tan[y]]],{x,-π/2, π/2},{y,-π/2, π
/2},RegionFunction→Function[{x,y,z},2<x^2+y^2<9]]
```

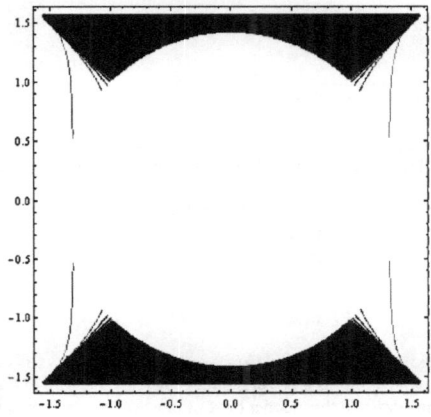

SYSTEM OF NONLINEAR EQUATIONS

In this part of the article we are going to develop some code to solve the system of nonlinear equations through extended Broyden method . The Broyden LUA codes are copyrighted by PAP and the extended Broyden method codes are copyrighted by the author of this article .

One of my friends with the nickname of Mohammad suggested me to extend the broyden method and use the Infinity applications that we discussed earlier in the method to have an improved method to solve the system of non-linear equations . After thinking about the method I could find an algorithm to find the solutions of the system of non-linear equations . First we will describe the Broyden method then we will extend it .

- **Broyden**[2]

The function Broyden solves a system of non-linear equations by implementing Broyden's method . This method is iterative, and tries to find a solution, starting by a user-supplied initial guess . It is often considered as the method of choice for solving systems of non-linear equations .

Syntax[2]

```
Root=Broyden(xguess,F,J,eps,maxit,show)
```

returns a vector root,which is the solution of a system of non-linear equations . The general form of a system of N non-linear equations with N unknowns $x_1, x_2, \ldots, x_N$ is F(x)=0 , which is expressed analytically as

$$F_1(x_1, x_2, \ldots, x_N) = 0$$
$$F_2(x_1, x_2, \ldots, x_N) = 0$$
$$\vdots$$
$$F_N(x_1, x_2, \ldots, x_N) = 0$$

Xguess is initial guess of the solution , and should be a vector of N elements . F is the name of a user-defined function F(x) , which returns a vector defining the left-hand-side of the equations to be solved , given a vector x defining the independent variables . The arguments **J,eps,maxit** , and **show** are optional .

The argument J must be the name of a function J(x) defining the Jacobian matrix J(x) . If omitted , this argument takes the default value J="auto" , which means that Jacobian will be computed numerically .

Eps defines the desired accuracy (default : **Epsilon** , i.e , 1.12×10^{-16}); **maxit** defines the maximum number of iterations (default : 20) ; **show** is a Boolean argument that controls whether progress of calculation will be displayed or not (default : **false**) .

Example [2]
Consider the system of non-linear equations
$$x_1 - x_2^4 + x_3 - 5 = 0$$
$$x_1^2 + x_2^3 - 3 = 0$$
$$x_1 + x_2 x_3^2 = 0$$

In this case , the multivariate function F(x) is defined as
$$F(x) = F(x_1, x_2, x_3) = \begin{bmatrix} x_1 - x_2^4 + x_3 - 5 \\ x_1^2 + x_2^3 - 3 \\ x_1 + x_2 x_3^2 \end{bmatrix}.$$

Its Jacobian is
$$J(x) = J(x_1, x_2, x_3) = \begin{bmatrix} 1 & -4x_2^3 & 1 \\ 2x_1 & 3x_2^2 & 0 \\ 1 & x_3^2 & 2x_1 x_2 \end{bmatrix}.$$

The example program **XBroyden** uses the function Broyden to find the solution of this system of non-linear equations with initial guess $x_1 = 2$, $x_2 = 0$, $x_3 = 3$. In order to check the result , the program computes the function values at the solution obtained .

```
require("LNA/Broyden")

local function F(x)
return {x[1]-x[2]^4+x[3]-5,x[1]^2+x[2]^3-3,x[1]+x[2]*x[3]^2}
end

local function J(x)
return {{1,-4*x[2]^3,1},{2*x[1],3*x[2]^2,0},{1,x[3]^2,2*x[2]*x[3]}}
end

local root

root=Broyden({2,0,3},F,J)
print("Solution:")
for i,v in ipairs(root) do print(i,v) end
print("\nFunction value:")
for i,v in ipairs(F(root)) do print(i,v) end
```

Example Program : XBroyden

The Figure bellow shows the results obtained by running this program . Note that , in this example , the Jacobian is defined by the user . Alternativley , one can call the function **Broyden** as **root=Broyden({2,0,3},F)** . In this case , the Jacobian is omitted , and it is computed numerically.

The reader should modify the initial guess in the above example , to see how the solution obtained is affected by a "bad" initial guess . For example , try following cases :
1. **xguess={3,1,6}** is not a good initial guess , but the solution obtained is correct .
2. **xguess={1,0,5}** is not a good initial guess , but the solution obtained is accurate , although the maximum number of iteration is reached , and the accuracy criterian is not satisfied .
3. **xguess={0,1,0}** is a very bad initial guess ; the maximum number of iteration is reached , the accuracy criterion is not satisfied ,and the "solution" obtained is wrong .

Remarks [2]
A good choice of initial guess **xguess** is crucial for Broyden's algorithm . Although you may get correct results using an initial guess far from the correct solution , it is always better to supply a good initial guess . Failure to do so may cause **Broyden** to return a totally wrong "solution" ; in this case , a nil value will be returned , and you should alter the initial guess.

Usually , there is no need to change the default value for "accuracy" **eps** . The algorithm should converge after a few iterations ; if it does not , it is almost sure that it will never converge ,

Results obtained by the example program **XBroyden** .

Due to wrong initial guess , or wrong input data . In other words , you will probably never need to use the optional argument maxit . The most common error when using **Broyden** is to define F incorrectly ; is most cases , this will cause wrong results , obtained after the maximum number of iterations is reached .

If the Jacobian is omitted , it is computed numerically by using the function Jacobian . Although numerical computation of the Jacobian is usually accurate enough , it is better to supply it by using the argument . In most cases , computing the Jacobian analytically is not difficult at all .

- **Extended Broyden Method**

Now we are going to develop the extended **Broyden** method to solve the system of non-linear equations to find the solutions of the system as the variables are varied in the Range $(-\infty, +\infty)$.

The **Broyden** method uses initial guesses . we can improve the method by increasing and decreasing the initial guesses in a domain of a transformed function. We will introduce the method through an example .

Assume that we have the following function (it is the example that we used for introducing the Broyden method in the previous section):

```
local function F(x)
return {x[1]-x[2]^4+x[3]-5,x[1]^2+x[2]^3-3,x[1]-x[2]*x[3]^2}
end
```

First we should transform the main function using the following Formula :

```
ArcTan(F(Tan(x)))
```

Then we should increase and decrease the variables that are included in the initial guesses just in the domain of $\left[-\frac{\pi}{2}, \frac{\pi}{2}\right]$.

The transformed function in lua code will be as follows :

```
local function FTrans(x)
return math.atan(F(math.tan(x)))
end
```

Instead of using **ArcTan** in the above code , we will use a power series representing the **ArcTan** function .The Mathematica code to represent **ArcTan** as a power series with good accuracy is as follows :

```
Normal[Series[ArcTan[x], {x, 0, 50}]]
```

The result will be:

$$F = \text{Function}[\{x\}, x - \frac{x^3}{3} + \frac{x^5}{5} - \frac{x^7}{7} + \frac{x^9}{9} - \frac{x^{11}}{11} + \frac{x^{13}}{13} - \frac{x^{15}}{15} + \frac{x^{17}}{17} - \frac{x^{19}}{19} + \frac{x^{21}}{21} - \frac{x^{23}}{23} + \frac{x^{25}}{25} - \frac{x^{27}}{27} + \frac{x^{29}}{29} - \frac{x^{31}}{31} + \frac{x^{33}}{33} - \frac{x^{35}}{35} + \frac{x^{37}}{37} - \frac{x^{39}}{39} + \frac{x^{41}}{41} - \frac{x^{43}}{43} + \frac{x^{45}}{45} - \frac{x^{47}}{47} + \frac{x^{49}}{49}]$$

So the terms of **Ftrans** function will be as follows :

Term 1 :

The mathematica Code to produce **Ftrans** term 1 is :

```
F[Tan[x[1]] - (Tan[x[2]])^4 + Tan[x[3]] - 5]
```

the result will be :

$$-5 + \text{Tan}[x[1]] - \text{Tan}[x[2]]^4 + \text{Tan}[x[3]] - \frac{1}{3}(-5 + \text{Tan}[x[1]] - \text{Tan}[x[2]]^4 + \text{Tan}[x[3]])^3$$
$$+ \frac{1}{5}(-5 + \text{Tan}[x[1]] - \text{Tan}[x[2]]^4 + \text{Tan}[x[3]])^5 - \frac{1}{7}(-5 + \text{Tan}[x[1]] - \text{Tan}[x[2]]^4 + \text{Tan}[x[3]])^7$$
$$+ \frac{1}{9}(-5 + \text{Tan}[x[1]] - \text{Tan}[x[2]]^4 + \text{Tan}[x[3]])^9 - \frac{1}{11}(-5 + \text{Tan}[x[1]] - \text{Tan}[x[2]]^4 + \text{Tan}[x[3]])^{11}$$
$$+ \frac{1}{13}(-5 + \text{Tan}[x[1]] - \text{Tan}[x[2]]^4 + \text{Tan}[x[3]])^{13} - \frac{1}{15}(-5 + \text{Tan}[x[1]] - \text{Tan}[x[2]]^4 + \text{Tan}[x[3]])^{15}$$
$$+ \frac{1}{17}(-5 + \text{Tan}[x[1]] - \text{Tan}[x[2]]^4 + \text{Tan}[x[3]])^{17} - \frac{1}{19}(-5 + \text{Tan}[x[1]] - \text{Tan}[x[2]]^4 + \text{Tan}[x[3]])^{19}$$
$$+ \frac{1}{21}(-5 + \text{Tan}[x[1]] - \text{Tan}[x[2]]^4 + \text{Tan}[x[3]])^{21} - \frac{1}{23}(-5 + \text{Tan}[x[1]] - \text{Tan}[x[2]]^4 + \text{Tan}[x[3]])^{23}$$
$$+ \frac{1}{25}(-5 + \text{Tan}[x[1]] - \text{Tan}[x[2]]^4 + \text{Tan}[x[3]])^{25} - \frac{1}{27}(-5 + \text{Tan}[x[1]] - \text{Tan}[x[2]]^4 + \text{Tan}[x[3]])^{27}$$
$$+ \frac{1}{29}(-5 + \text{Tan}[x[1]] - \text{Tan}[x[2]]^4 + \text{Tan}[x[3]])^{29} - \frac{1}{31}(-5 + \text{Tan}[x[1]] - \text{Tan}[x[2]]^4 + \text{Tan}[x[3]])^{31}$$
$$+ \frac{1}{33}(-5 + \text{Tan}[x[1]] - \text{Tan}[x[2]]^4 + \text{Tan}[x[3]])^{33} - \frac{1}{35}(-5 + \text{Tan}[x[1]] - \text{Tan}[x[2]]^4 + \text{Tan}[x[3]])^{35}$$
$$+ \frac{1}{37}(-5 + \text{Tan}[x[1]] - \text{Tan}[x[2]]^4 + \text{Tan}[x[3]])^{37} - \frac{1}{39}(-5 + \text{Tan}[x[1]] - \text{Tan}[x[2]]^4 + \text{Tan}[x[3]])^{39}$$
$$+ \frac{1}{41}(-5 + \text{Tan}[x[1]] - \text{Tan}[x[2]]^4 + \text{Tan}[x[3]])^{41} - \frac{1}{43}(-5 + \text{Tan}[x[1]] - \text{Tan}[x[2]]^4 + \text{Tan}[x[3]])^{43}$$
$$+ \frac{1}{45}(-5 + \text{Tan}[x[1]] - \text{Tan}[x[2]]^4 + \text{Tan}[x[3]])^{45} - \frac{1}{47}(-5 + \text{Tan}[x[1]] - \text{Tan}[x[2]]^4 + \text{Tan}[x[3]])^{47}$$
$$+ \frac{1}{49}(-5 + \text{Tan}[x[1]] - \text{Tan}[x[2]]^4 + \text{Tan}[x[3]])^{49}$$

Term 2 :

The mathematica Code to produce **Ftrans** term 2 is :

```
F[(Tan[x[1]])^2 - (Tan[x[2]])^3 - 3]
```

the result will be :

$$-3 + \text{Tan}[x[1]]^2 - \text{Tan}[x[2]]^3 - \frac{1}{3}(-3 + \text{Tan}[x[1]]^2 - \text{Tan}[x[2]]^3)^3 + \frac{1}{5}(-3 + \text{Tan}[x[1]]^2 - \text{Tan}[x[2]]^3)^5$$
$$- \frac{1}{7}(-3 + \text{Tan}[x[1]]^2 - \text{Tan}[x[2]]^3)^7 + \frac{1}{9}(-3 + \text{Tan}[x[1]]^2 - \text{Tan}[x[2]]^3)^9$$
$$- \frac{1}{11}(-3 + \text{Tan}[x[1]]^2 - \text{Tan}[x[2]]^3)^{11} + \frac{1}{13}(-3 + \text{Tan}[x[1]]^2 - \text{Tan}[x[2]]^3)^{13}$$
$$- \frac{1}{15}(-3 + \text{Tan}[x[1]]^2 - \text{Tan}[x[2]]^3)^{15} + \frac{1}{17}(-3 + \text{Tan}[x[1]]^2 - \text{Tan}[x[2]]^3)^{17}$$
$$- \frac{1}{19}(-3 + \text{Tan}[x[1]]^2 - \text{Tan}[x[2]]^3)^{19} + \frac{1}{21}(-3 + \text{Tan}[x[1]]^2 - \text{Tan}[x[2]]^3)^{21}$$
$$- \frac{1}{23}(-3 + \text{Tan}[x[1]]^2 - \text{Tan}[x[2]]^3)^{23} + \frac{1}{25}(-3 + \text{Tan}[x[1]]^2 - \text{Tan}[x[2]]^3)^{25}$$
$$- \frac{1}{27}(-3 + \text{Tan}[x[1]]^2 - \text{Tan}[x[2]]^3)^{27} + \frac{1}{29}(-3 + \text{Tan}[x[1]]^2 - \text{Tan}[x[2]]^3)^{29}$$
$$- \frac{1}{31}(-3 + \text{Tan}[x[1]]^2 - \text{Tan}[x[2]]^3)^{31} + \frac{1}{33}(-3 + \text{Tan}[x[1]]^2 - \text{Tan}[x[2]]^3)^{33}$$
$$- \frac{1}{35}(-3 + \text{Tan}[x[1]]^2 - \text{Tan}[x[2]]^3)^{35} + \frac{1}{37}(-3 + \text{Tan}[x[1]]^2 - \text{Tan}[x[2]]^3)^{37}$$
$$- \frac{1}{39}(-3 + \text{Tan}[x[1]]^2 - \text{Tan}[x[2]]^3)^{39} + \frac{1}{41}(-3 + \text{Tan}[x[1]]^2 - \text{Tan}[x[2]]^3)^{41}$$
$$- \frac{1}{43}(-3 + \text{Tan}[x[1]]^2 - \text{Tan}[x[2]]^3)^{43} + \frac{1}{45}(-3 + \text{Tan}[x[1]]^2 - \text{Tan}[x[2]]^3)^{45}$$
$$- \frac{1}{47}(-3 + \text{Tan}[x[1]]^2 - \text{Tan}[x[2]]^3)^{47} + \frac{1}{49}(-3 + \text{Tan}[x[1]]^2 - \text{Tan}[x[2]]^3)^{49}$$

Term 3 :
The mathematica Code to produce **Ftrans** term 3 is :

```
F[(Tan[x[1]])^2 - (Tan[x[2]])^3 - 3]
```

the result will be :

$$\text{Tan}[x[1]] + \text{Tan}[x[2]]\text{Tan}[x[3]]^2 - \frac{1}{3}(\text{Tan}[x[1]] + \text{Tan}[x[2]]\text{Tan}[x[3]]^2)^3 + \frac{1}{5}(\text{Tan}[x[1]] + \text{Tan}[x[2]]\text{Tan}[x[3]]^2)^5$$
$$- \frac{1}{7}(\text{Tan}[x[1]] + \text{Tan}[x[2]]\text{Tan}[x[3]]^2)^7 + \frac{1}{9}(\text{Tan}[x[1]] + \text{Tan}[x[2]]\text{Tan}[x[3]]^2)^9$$
$$- \frac{1}{11}(\text{Tan}[x[1]] + \text{Tan}[x[2]]\text{Tan}[x[3]]^2)^{11} + \frac{1}{13}(\text{Tan}[x[1]] + \text{Tan}[x[2]]\text{Tan}[x[3]]^2)^{13}$$
$$- \frac{1}{15}(\text{Tan}[x[1]] + \text{Tan}[x[2]]\text{Tan}[x[3]]^2)^{15} + \frac{1}{17}(\text{Tan}[x[1]] + \text{Tan}[x[2]]\text{Tan}[x[3]]^2)^{17}$$
$$- \frac{1}{19}(\text{Tan}[x[1]] + \text{Tan}[x[2]]\text{Tan}[x[3]]^2)^{19} + \frac{1}{21}(\text{Tan}[x[1]] + \text{Tan}[x[2]]\text{Tan}[x[3]]^2)^{21}$$
$$- \frac{1}{23}(\text{Tan}[x[1]] + \text{Tan}[x[2]]\text{Tan}[x[3]]^2)^{23} + \frac{1}{25}(\text{Tan}[x[1]] + \text{Tan}[x[2]]\text{Tan}[x[3]]^2)^{25}$$
$$- \frac{1}{27}(\text{Tan}[x[1]] + \text{Tan}[x[2]]\text{Tan}[x[3]]^2)^{27} + \frac{1}{29}(\text{Tan}[x[1]] + \text{Tan}[x[2]]\text{Tan}[x[3]]^2)^{29}$$
$$- \frac{1}{31}(\text{Tan}[x[1]] + \text{Tan}[x[2]]\text{Tan}[x[3]]^2)^{31} + \frac{1}{33}(\text{Tan}[x[1]] + \text{Tan}[x[2]]\text{Tan}[x[3]]^2)^{33}$$
$$- \frac{1}{35}(\text{Tan}[x[1]] + \text{Tan}[x[2]]\text{Tan}[x[3]]^2)^{35} + \frac{1}{37}(\text{Tan}[x[1]] + \text{Tan}[x[2]]\text{Tan}[x[3]]^2)^{37}$$
$$- \frac{1}{39}(\text{Tan}[x[1]] + \text{Tan}[x[2]]\text{Tan}[x[3]]^2)^{39} + \frac{1}{41}(\text{Tan}[x[1]] + \text{Tan}[x[2]]\text{Tan}[x[3]]^2)^{41}$$
$$- \frac{1}{43}(\text{Tan}[x[1]] + \text{Tan}[x[2]]\text{Tan}[x[3]]^2)^{43} + \frac{1}{45}(\text{Tan}[x[1]] + \text{Tan}[x[2]]\text{Tan}[x[3]]^2)^{45}$$
$$- \frac{1}{47}(\text{Tan}[x[1]] + \text{Tan}[x[2]]\text{Tan}[x[3]]^2)^{47} + \frac{1}{49}(\text{Tan}[x[1]] + \text{Tan}[x[2]]\text{Tan}[x[3]]^2)^{49}$$

In this example we have 3 variables and each variable can increase or decrease in the domain of $\left[-\frac{\pi}{2},\frac{\pi}{2}\right]$.

So we will have 3 loops that in the first loop X[1] variable will be changed in the domain $\left[-\frac{\pi}{2},\frac{\pi}{2}\right]$ with the user defined step (accuracy) and X[2] and X[3] will be $-\frac{\pi}{2}$ and in the second loop X[2] will be changed in the domain $\left[-\frac{\pi}{2},\frac{\pi}{2}\right]$ while X[3] is $-\frac{\pi}{2}$ and X[1] will be changed in the domain $\left[-\frac{\pi}{2},\frac{\pi}{2}\right]$ for each X[2] value and in the last loop X[3] will be changed in the domain $\left[-\frac{\pi}{2},\frac{\pi}{2}\right]$ while X[2] will be changed in the domain $\left[-\frac{\pi}{2},\frac{\pi}{2}\right]$ for each X[3] value and X[1] will be changed in the domain $\left[-\frac{\pi}{2},\frac{\pi}{2}\right]$ for each X[2] value .

In each loop we will see if the try will converge to a solution with satisfied accuracy or not . If the solution is converged with satisfied accuracy we will use the result as a good initial guess for the **Broyden** method with the main function . when we reach to the end of first loop the next loop will be started and we will continue upto the end of the procedure .

In this method the solutions for the **Ftrans** function will be the initial guesses for the F function .

Using this method the real solutions of the system of equations with each variable varied in the domain $(-\infty, +\infty)$ will be optained .

Syntax

BroyINF(nvar,F,Ftrans,step,J,Jtrans,eps,maxit,show)

Returns a vector root , which is the solution of a system of non-linear equations . The general form of a system of N non-linear equations with N unknowns $x_1, x_2, \dots, x_N$ is F(x)=0 , which is expressed analytically as

$$F_1(x_1, x_2, \dots, x_N) = 0$$
$$F_2(x_1, x_2, \dots, x_N) = 0$$
$$\cdot \quad \cdot \quad \cdot$$
$$\cdot \quad \cdot \quad \cdot$$
$$F_N(x_1, x_2, \dots, x_N) = 0$$

nvar is the maximum number of variables is the equations . **F** is the name of a user-defined function F(x) , which returns a vector defining the left hand side of the equations to be solved , given a vector x defining the independent variables . **Ftrans** is the transformed function of F using the following transformation .

> ArcTan(F(Tan(x)))

step is the step size in the solution, can be started from 0.01 to the **Epsilon**. smaller step size take more time to solve the system of equations and more results may be found.

The arguments **J**, **Jtrans**, **eps**, **maxit** and **show** are optional.
The argument **J** must be the name of a function J(x) defining the Jacobian matrix J(x). If omitted, this argument takes the default value **J="auto"**, which means that Jacobian will be computed numerically.
The argument **Jtrans** must be the name of a function Jtrans(x) defining the Jacobian matrix Jtrans(x). If omitted, this argument takes the default value **Jtrans="auto"**, which means that Jacobian of the transformed function will be computed numerically.

Eps defines the desired accuracy (default : **Epsilon**, i.e , 1.12×10^{-16}); **maxit** defines the maximum number of iterations (default : 20) ; **show** is a Boolean argument that controls whether progress of calculation will be displayed or not (default : **false**).

Example Driver program
The Driver program to solve the example will be as follows :

```
require("LNA/BroyINF")

local function F(x)
return {x[1]-x[2]^4+x[3]-5,x[1]^2+x[2]^3-3,x[1]+x[2]*x[3]^2}
end

local function Ftransformer(x)
return
x-x^3/3+x^5/5-x^7/7+x^9/9-x^11/11+x^13/13-x^15/15+x^17/17-x^19/19+x^21/21-
x^23/23+x^25/25-x^27/27+x^29/29-x^31/31+x^33/33-x^35/35+x^37/37-x^39/39+x^41/41-
x^43/43+x^45/45-x^47/47+x^49/49
end

local function Ftrans(x)
return
{Ftransformer(F({math.tan(x[1]),math.tan(x[2]),math.tan(x[3])})[1]),Ftransformer(F({math.tan(x[
1]),math.tan(x[2]),math.tan(x[3])})[2]),Ftransformer(F({math.tan(x[1]),math.tan(x[2]),math.tan(
x[3])})[3])}
end

BroyINF(3,F,Ftrans,0.3)
```

The results will be as follows :

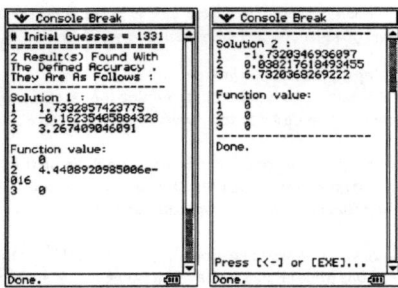

The Extended Broyden method Code and its requirements :

BroyINF

```
require("table","LNAutils/Epsilon","LNAutils/Pi","LNAutils/MatMul","LNAutils/MatTrans","LNA/Jacobia","LNA/LUdecom","LNA/Broyden")

function BroyINF(nvar,F,Ftrans,step,...)
local J="auto"
local Jtrans="auto"
local eps=Epsilon
local maxit=20
local show=false
if arg["n"]>=1 then
 J=arg[1]
 if arn["n"]>=2 then
  Jtrans=arg[2]
  if arg["n"]>=3 then
   eps=arg[3]
   if arg["n"]>=4 then
    maxit=arg[4]
    if arg["n"]>=5 then
```

```
    show=arg[5]
   end
  end
 end
 end
end

local n=nvar
local stepi=1

local xguessvalue = {}
if (n == 1) then
   for a11=-Pi/2,Pi/2,step do
      xguessvalue[stepi] = {a11}
  stepi=stepi+1
   end
end


if (n == 2) then
   for a12=-Pi/2,Pi/2,step do
      for a11=-Pi/2,Pi/2,step do
         xguessvalue[stepi] = {a11, a12}
   stepi=stepi+1
     end
   end
end


if (n == 3) then
   for a13=-Pi/2,Pi/2,step do
     for a12=-Pi/2,Pi/2,step do
       for a11=-Pi/2,Pi/2,step do
          xguessvalue[stepi] = {a11, a12, a13}
   stepi=stepi+1
         end
      end
   end
end


if (n == 4) then
   for a14=-Pi/2,Pi/2,step do
     for a13=-Pi/2,Pi/2,step do
       for a12=-Pi/2,Pi/2,step do
         for a11=-Pi/2,Pi/2,step do
```

```
            xguessvalue[stepi] = {a11, a12, a13, a14}
    stepi=stepi+1
          end
        end
      end
    end
end

if (n==5) then
  for a15=-Pi/2,Pi/2,step do
    for a14=-Pi/2,Pi/2,step do
      for a13=-Pi/2,Pi/2,step do
        for a12=-Pi/2,Pi/2,step do
          for a11=-Pi/2,Pi/2,step do
            xguessvalue[stepi] = {a11, a12, a13, a14}
    stepi=stepi+1
          end
        end
      end
    end
  end
end


lengthguess=stepi-1
print("# Initial Guesses = "..lengthguess)
local root={}
local solution={}
local solutionc={}
for ii = 1,lengthguess do
   solution[ii]=Broyden(xguessvalue[ii],Ftrans,Jtrans)
     if (solution[ii] ~=nil) then
       solutionc = {};
       for i=1,n do
         solutionc[i]=math.tan(solution[ii][i]);
       end
   root[ii]=Broyden(solutionc,F,J,eps,maxit,show)

     else

        root[ii]=nil
     end
end
```

```
result = {};
resulti = 0;
mresult = {};
stepi2last = stepi-1;

for steppass2i=1,stepi2last do
   for m=1,(2^n) do
      if root[steppass2i]~=nil then
         pvalue = 0;
         for steppass3i=1,steppass2i do
            if (steppass3i ~= steppass2i ) then
               mprocess = (2^n)
            else
               mprocess = m;
            end
            for m2=1,mprocess do
               pkey = 0;
               if root[steppass3i]~=nil then
                  for i=1,n do
                     if(math.abs(root[steppass2i][i] - root[steppass3i][i]) < 0.0000000001) then
                        pkey = pkey + 1
                     end
                  end
               end
               if (pkey == n) then
                  pvalue = pvalue + 1
               end
            end
         end
         if (pvalue == 1) then
            resulti = resulti + 1
            result[resulti]=steppass2i
            mresult[resulti]=m
         end
      end
   end
end


print("=====================")
if resulti==0 then
 print("No Result Found With The Defined Accuracy")
else
```

```
print(resulti.." Result(s) Found With The Defined Accuracy . They Are As Follows :")
print("----------------------")
for istep=1,resulti do
 print("Solution "..istep.." :")
 for i,v in ipairs(root[result[istep]]) do print(i,v) end
 print("\nFunction value:")
 for i,v in ipairs(F(root[result[istep]])) do print(i,v) end
 print("----------------------")
 end
end



end

export{BroyINF=BroyINF}
```

Broyden

```
require("table","LNAutils/Epsilon","LNAutils/MatMul","LNAutils/MatTrans","LNA/Jacobia","LNA
/LUdecom")

function Broyden(xguess,F,...)
local J="auto"
local eps=Epsilon
local maxit=20
local show=false
if arg["n"]>=1 then
 J=arg[1]
 if arg["n"]>=2 then
  eps=arg[2]
  if arg["n"]>=3 then
   maxit=arg[3]
   if arg["n"]>=4 then
    show=arg[4]
   end
  end
 end
end
--Numerical Jacobian:
if J=="auto" then
 local function Jnum(x)
  return Jacobian(F,x)
```

```
  end
  J=Jnum
 end
 --Local variables:
 local n=#xguess
 local LU,indx,v,vmax,Fcur,Fpre,Ainv,Ainvy,DTAinv,DTAinvy,DmAinvy,aux
 local y={}
 local DmAinvy={}
 local x=table.copy(xguess)
 --First root estimation:
 Fpre=F(x)
 LU,indx=LUdecompose(J(x))
 Ainv=LUinverse(LU,indx)
 v=MatMul(Ainv,Fpre)
 for i=1,n do
  x[i]=x[i]-v[i]
 end
 if show then
  print(" i  max discrepancy")
  vmax=math.abs(v[1])
  for i=2,n do
   aux=math.abs(v[i])
   if aux>vmax then
   vmax=aux end
  end
  printf("%2i  %e\n",1,vmax)
 end
 for iter=2,maxit do
  --Jacobian inverse:
  Fcur=F(x)
  for i=1,n do
   y[i]=Fcur[i]-Fpre[i]
  end
  Ainvy=MatMul(Ainv,y)
  DTAinv=MatMul(v,Ainv)
  for i=1,n do
   DmAinvy[i]=-v[i]-Ainvy[i]
  end
  aux=MatMul(MatTrans(DmAinvy),{DTAinv})
  DTAinvy=MatMul(DTAinv,y)
  for i=1,n do
   for j=1,n do
    Ainv[i][j]=Ainv[i][j]+aux[i][j]/DTAinvy
   end
  end
  --Next root estimation:
```

```
v=MatMul(Ainv,Fcur)
for i=1,n do
 x[i]=x[i]-v[i]
end
--Loop or return:
vmax=math.abs(v[1])
for i=2,n do
 aux=math.abs(v[i])
 if aux>vmax then
  vmax=aux end
end
if show then
 printf("%2i  %e\n",iter,vmax)
end
if vmax<eps then
 return x
else
 Fpre=Fcur
end
end
--Return with warning:

return nil
end

export{Broyden=Broyden}
```

Epsilon

```
Epsilon=1.12E-16
export{Epsilon=Epsilon}
```

LNAutils/MatMul

```
require("LNAutils/MatCol","LNAutils/MatTrans")
function MatMul(A,B)
local C={}
local rowA,colA,rowB,colB
if type(A[1])=="number" then
 A={A}
```

```
end
rowB=#B
if type(B[1])=="number" then
 B=MatTrans(B);colB=1
else
 colB=#B[1]
end
rowA=#A;colA=#A[1]
if colA~=rowB then
 print("Error: MatMul: Undefined matrix multiplication.")
 return nil
end
for i=1,rowA do
 C[i]={}
 for j=1,colB do
  C[i][j]=0
  for k=1,colA do
   C[i][j]=C[i][j]+A[i][k]*B[k][j]
  end
 end
end
if colB==1 then
 C=MatCol(C,1)
end

if rowA==1 then
 C=C[1]
end
return C
end
export{MatMul=MatMul}
```

LNAutils/MatCol

```
function MatCol(A,col)
local C={}
if type(A[1])=="table" then
 for row=1,#A do
  C[row]=A[row][col]
 end
else
 C[1]=A[col]
```

```
end
return C
end

export{MatCol=MatCol}
```

LNAutils/MatTrans

```
require("LNAutils/MatCol")
function MatTrans(M)
local Mt={}
local cols
if type(M[1])=="table" then cols=#M[1]
else cols=#M end
for i=1,cols do
 Mt[i]=MatCol(M,i)
end
return Mt
end
export{MatTrans=MatTrans}
```

LNA/Jacobia

```
require("table")
function Jacobian(F,x)
local n=#x
local Fx=F(x)
local dx={}
local Fxk={}
local xaux
local J={}
for k=1,n do
 if x[k]~=0 then
  dx[k]=1E-8*x[k]
 else
  dx[k]=1E-8
 end
 xaux=table.copy(x)
 xaux[k]=x[k]+dx[k]
```

```
  Fxk[k]=F(xaux)
 end
 for i=1,n do
  J[i]={}
  for k=1,n do
   J[i][k]=(Fxk[k][i]-Fx[i])/dx[k]
  end
 end
 return J
end

export{Jacobian=Jacobian}
```

LNA/ LUdecom

```
require("table","LNAutils/MatCol","LNAutils/MatIdent","LNAutils/MatTrans")
function LUdecompose(A)
 local LU={}
 local indx={}
 local parity=1
 local n=table.getn(A)
 local p,Dp,Dc,aux
 for i=1,n do
  LU[i]=table.copy(A[i])
  indx[i]=i
 end
 for j=1,n-1 do
  --Upper triangular:
  for i=1,j do
   for k=1,i-1 do
    LU[i][j]=LU[i][j]-LU[i][k]*LU[k][j]
   end
  end
  --Lower triangular:
  for i=j+1,n do
   for k=1,j-1 do
    LU[i][j]=LU[i][j]-LU[i][k]*LU[k][j]
   end
  end
  --Pivoting:
  p=j
  Dp=math.abs(LU[p][j])
  for i=j+1,n do
```

```
    Dc=math.abs(LU[i][j])
    if Dc>Dp then
     p=i;Dp=Dc
    end
   end
   if Dp==0 then
    print("Warning: LUdecompose: Singular matrix.")
    return nil,nil,nil
   end
   --Permutation:
   if p~=j then
    for k=1,n do
     LU[j][k],LU[p][k]=LU[p][k],LU[j][k]
    end
    indx[j],indx[p]=indx[p],indx[j]
    parity=-parity
   end
   --Sub-diagonal division:
   aux=LU[j][j]
   for i=j+1,n do
    LU[i][j]=LU[i][j]/aux
   end
  end
  --Last column:
  for i=1,n do
   for k=1,i-1 do
    LU[i][n]=LU[i][n]-LU[i][k]*LU[k][n]
   end
  end
  return LU,indx,parity
 end
 function LUsubstitute(LU,indx,B)
  local X={}
  local Z={}
  local n,s
  if LU~=nil then
   n=table.getn(indx)

   --Lower system solution:
   Z[1]=B[indx[1]]
   for i=2,n do
    s=0
    for k=1,i-1 do
     s=s+LU[i][k]*Z[k]
    end
    Z[i]=B[indx[i]]-s
```

```
    end
  --Upper system solution:
  X[n]=Z[n]/LU[n][n]
  for i=n-1,1,-1 do
   s=0
   for k=i+1,n do
    s=s+LU[i][k]*X[k]
   end
   X[i]=(Z[i]-s)/LU[i][i]
  end
  return X
 else
  return nil
 end
end

function LUdeterminant(LU,parity)
 local s=1
 if LU~=nil then
  for i=1,table.getn(LU) do
   s=s*LU[i][i]
  end
  return parity*s
 else
  return 0
 end
end
function LUinverse(LU,indx)
 local Ainv={}
 local n,Id
 if LU~=nil then
  n=table.getn(LU)
  Id=MatIdent(n)
  for i=1,n do
   Ainv[i]=LUsubstitute(LU,indx,MatCol(Id,i))
  end
  return MatTrans(Ainv)
 else
  return nil
 end
end

function LUsolve(A,B)
 local X,LU,indx,parity
 LU,indx,parity=LUdecompose(A)
 X=LUsubstitute(LU,indx,B)
```

```
return X
end
export{LUsolve=LUsolve,LUdecompose=LUdecompose,LUsubstitute=LUsubstitute,LUdeterminant
=LUdeterminant,LUinverse=LUinverse}
```

```
LNAutils/MatIdent
```

```
function MatIdent(n)
local I={}
for i=1,n do
 I[i]={}
 for j=1,n do
  I[i][j]=0
 end
 I[i][i]=1
end
return I
end
export{MatIdent=MatIdent}
```

Another Example

In this example we will have a function with 2 variable . The function is :

```
local function F(x)
return {x[1]-x[2]^2+5,x[1]-math.sin(x[2])}
end
```

The Driver program

```
require("LNA/BroyINF")

local function F(x)
return {x[1]-x[2]^2+5,x[1]-math.sin(x[2])}
end

local function Ftransformer(x)
return
```

```
x-x^3/3+x^5/5-x^7/7+x^9/9-x^11/11+x^13/13-x^15/15+x^17/17-x^19/19+x^21/21-
x^23/23+x^25/25-x^27/27+x^29/29-x^31/31+x^33/33-x^35/35+x^37/37-x^39/39+x^41/41-
x^43/43+x^45/45-x^47/47+x^49/49
end


local function Ftrans(x)
return
{Ftransformer(F({math.tan(x[1]),math.tan(x[2])})[1]),Ftransformer(F({math.tan(x[1]),math.tan(x[
2])})[2])}
end


BroyINF(2,F,Ftrans,0.1)
```

Results

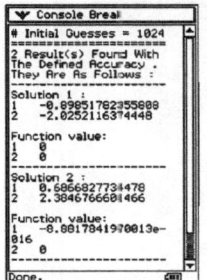

Checking the result through Mathematica :

```
FindRoot[{y == (x)^2 - 5, y == Sin[x]}, {{x, 2}, {y, 1}}]
FindRoot[{y == (x)^2 - 5, y == Sin[x]}, {{x, -2}, {y, -1}}]
```

Result :

```
{x -> 2.38468, y -> 0.686683}
{x -> -2.02521, y -> -0.898518}
```

Plotting the functions using Mathematica:

```
Plot[{ArcTan[(Tan[x])^2 - 5],ArcTan[Sin[Tan[x]]]}, {x, -([Pi]/2), [Pi]/2},PlotRange -> [Pi]/2]
```

Result :

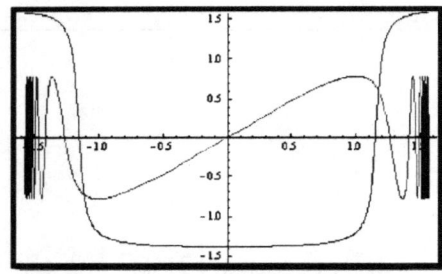

REFERENCES

[1] Mathematica Book , Version 5.1
Author : Stephen Wolfram , Wolfram Research Institute

[2] LNA "Lua Numerical Analysis" , Programmer's Manual ,Version 1.6
Author : PAP